Randy King

Chef in the *Wild*

Reflections and recipes from a true wilderness chef

bwc

Caxton Press

First Edition

Library of Congress Cataloging-in-Publication Data

King, Randy.
Chef in the wild : reflections and recipes from a true wilderness chef / by Randy King.
179 pages cm
Includes bibliographical references and index.
ISBN 978-0-87004-592-9 (alk. paper)
1. Cooking (Wild foods) 2. Hunting--Anecdotes. I. Title.

TX751.K48 2015
641.3'06--dc23

2015007325

Cover and book design by Jocelyn Robertson

Lithographed and bound in the United States of America
CAXTON PRESS
Caldwell, Idaho
189664

More praise for
CHEF in the WILD

"Every sunrise and sunset Randy King has lived the wild life. It shows in his love and passion for creating something special from what the land, air and water has given him." *Jesse Morris, KillerChefs*

"Randy King is a well-known chef of wild game, so I wasn't surprised by the creative style and original slant found in his recipes. What surprised and delighted me when reading Randy's *Chef in the Wild* were Randy's stories and reminiscing. In humorous and insightful style, he offers profound lessons based on his personal experiences and observations gleaned from years of hunting and fishing in the wild." *Darcy Williamson*, author of *The Rocky Mountains Wild Foods Cookbook*

"Randy has brought us back in time, so we can enjoy the labors of his parents and their doctrine of eating sustainable food. Thank you for this book Randy, we are in your debt for reminding us how we need to live." *Steve Weston*, author of *Outdoor Cookbook*

"Randy's book combines the best of both worlds – the thrill of the pursuit, and the tasty rewards of the harvest. Editing his stories for publication in *Northwest Sportsman* magazine these past several years has resulted in a permanent drool stain on my desk. Combining fishing and hunting tips with humor and pathos, he's created a memorable collection of wild game deliciousness." *Andy Walgamott*, Editor of *Northwest Sportsman* magazine

"Randy is like Alton Brown with a shotgun." *Alan Turner, Chef, AB Foods*

"*Chef in the Wild* speaks directly to the heart of the outdoorsmen or outdoorswomen in us all with narratives of adventure, camaraderie, danger, and excitement, which paint a picture of the journey wild food makes to the fork. The recipes convey a life and passion of food that honor the animal from whence it came and will call out to the stomach of any person who admires a real, properly prepared meal from the wild." *Justin Townsend, Harvesting Nature*

"*Chef in the Wild* is filled with easy, creative wild game recipes for the average home cook. King's personal anecdotes of his days afield with family and friends are fun and memorable reads." *Rick and Jen, Food for Hunters*

For Dad –
my love of wild places and wild food,
I owe to you.

Table of Contents

LAND

WATER

HOME

Introduction

It's a cool fall morning with fog hanging over Dave Shenk's farm in Homedale, Idaho. As I walk I can feel the weight of my ammunition in my shooting vest pressing against my shoulders and the tail feathers from a rooster pheasant poking me in the back. My legs are stiff from walking for hours through muddy fields, tilled under beans. But I have a hard time not smiling. My father flanks me on the left and my older brother on the right. This hunt is a family affair.

More than beans grow on Dave's farm. He also raises quail, partridges, deer, ducks and the pheasants I love to shoot on his land. While his crop might get sold on the market, his wildlife often ends up in a sauté pan feeding my family.

About 30 yards ahead the tops of the thistle bushes are moving, but no dog is visible. Miley, my dog, is somewhere in the weeds. I know her nose is down sniffing out the ever-elusive rooster. She is on the hunt.

The weeds stop moving and my muscles instinctively tense; Miley has probably found a bird. With a quick flurry, I hear a cackle and a rooster pheasant jumps into the air. I pull up and disengage the safety on my shotgun. The bird flies directly away from me as I pull the trigger, pump, and then pull again; my practiced movements are smooth and effortless. I stare in amazement as the bird continues to fly away.

To my left side I hear a single shot and watch the rooster fall to the ground. I turn to the canal bank and see my dad smiling at me; he's outshot me again. It's a tradition – one I am not a fan of – though in thirty years I hope to be outshooting my children.

Miley is right on top of the bird as it hits the ground. She stares at me and gums it in her mouth; she is not trained enough to bring the pheasant back to the shooter. I encourage her to fetch the bird but she just looks at me stupidly, like the house pet she really is.

Who shoots the bird or if the dog retrieves it are of little consequence; the hunting is a means to an end, an enjoyable excuse for a delicious meal. Our real goal is Mom's Pheasant Noodle Soup, a heavily-seasoned concoction that my family has been enjoying since before I can remember. It is a homestyle recipe that has been passed on to my mother and now to my sister and me. Soon enough, I will teach my sons to make it – one is just now old enough to hunt. This recipe is one of the main reasons I chose to cook for a living; it showed me from an early age that food could truly make people happy.

As I pick up the bird from in front of my dog, I hear the sound of my father's phone ringing in his pocket. Slipping the bird into the back of his vest, I hear him get excited. Two of his sisters are joining us for dinner. We need to shoot another pheasant!

Before dinnertime we skin and gut the birds. We take special care to wash the meat several times, since blood can cloud the soup broth. The next step is to slowly poach the bird until it is fall-off-the-bone tender. We remove it from the stock and let it cool. In a large pot, we place the Holy Trinity of Western cooking: mirepoix – two parts onion, one part carrot and one part celery – then lightly sauté this mix and add the pheasant broth. The mixture is brought to a simmer.

Trying not to eat too much as we go, we'll pick apart and shred the meat of the bird. The meat is added to the broth and left to simmer. Other game may come out of the freezer to add to the soup – like quail, cottontail rabbits and Hungarian partridges.

The egg noodles come next and they are, aside from the pheasant, the best part of the dish. The recipe is simple: a dough made of eggs, flour, salt and a little bit of cold water, rolled and cut into thin, fettuccini-sized noodles. The noodles plump up like dumplings in the broth and the soup is finished with fresh herbs like sage and parsley. The smell and taste is that of a deep, rich chicken noodle soup but with a distinct "wildness" to it.

Nothing fills my soul like sitting around the dinner table with three generations of Kings eating a big bowl of pheasant noodle soup; the smiling, the laughing, the two front teeth missing from my middle son. We are noodle soup folk, a generation of country people who have spent our lives hunting, cooking and eating wild game. As the cliché goes – we are what we eat.

My family makes the best of what nature provides. In times past most Americans could step out into the field behind the house and get a bird for dinner. They would go to the creek and catch a few trout for lunch. This was a reality as recently as a generation ago, when most of us still lived closer to nature – it is still a reality for my family. My father grew up hunting a majority of the meat he ate; in keeping with that tradition. I now choose to only eat wild game meat. I don't need to. I want to.

Hunting is controversial – hunters are familiar with nasty looks from neighbors and turned up noses from those who think of hunting as cruel. Large "No Hunting" signs mark private land. Some preach that humanity has moved beyond the need to hunt, beyond the need to shoot and kill.

Honestly, they are right. I do not need to hunt and kill to feed my family. I can buy all that we need at the store. Soulless meat widgets. Wrapped and processed in a USDA facility that is sanitary and cold. But I'd still be killing for food, just by proxy instead; someone else would hold the death in their hands.

The true nature of the world does not show itself in the refrigerated section of the grocery store. Hunters are seen as cruel only because of the distance our modern lives allow us from food production. But an image is an image, and hunters need to face up to how we are perceived. We must shed the Elmer Fudd stereotype that has cursed us for so long. The easiest way to show just how wonderful the hunting lifestyle can be is through food.

Luckily wild game is inherently delectable. It is also right on trend with the push for grass fed, hormone-free, cage-free, free-range, antibiotic-free, sustainable and organic foods. As such, hunters should strive for a balance that shows that we are stewards of the land working toward a sustainable lifestyle. Foodies and hunters need to unite, as disparate as they might seem on the surface. Hunter's orange should be worn as a badge of honor, for orange is the new green.

For those who don't hunt, I just ask that you keep an open mind. It is only in the modern age that we can even question the act of hunting. Only recently has humanity had the choice not to hunt. As a species we have spent 99.9% of our existence being hunters. The human form is designed to hunt – eyes forward, amazing distance running ability, unique ability to sweat off heat and our large problem-solving brains – all things evolved to make us more efficient at getting meat in our bellies. We are, evolutionarily speaking, designed to be hunters. To hunt is to be human.

I embrace this humanity. Sure, I do not need to hunt. I also do not need to eat organic, free-range, grass-fed, local and sustainable wild game. But I still feel a need that goes beyond all practicality, a need to hunt. For me, and many others, hunting and ethical eating are one and the same. I hunt, fish, and eat what I kill. Yes, I said kill – not harvest or take, but kill. What I do has a moral implication, as taking any flesh should.

And flesh is what this book is about: responsibly using a resource to fuel our minds, bodies, and souls. Hunting and fishing, for me, are about nourishment. Walking the cornrows and the woods nourishes my soul, what I bring home nourishes my body; the meditative state I reach hunting nourishes my mind.

I hunt for more than food, to be honest. I hunt for the adventure and joy of the chase – the heart racing anticipation of a flock of quail about to bust, the tug of a fish on my line, the buck that I know is right over the next ridge. I get more than calories out of my journeys. I hunt for meat and I hunt for more than meat.

But when the buck is down on the ground, the pheasant is in the hand, the catfish is on the stringer – what next?

It is at this point when I see others lock up, frozen with fear. They have worked so hard at getting the game animal – blood, sweat, sleepless nights, endless hours scouting, planning, packing, cutting, wrapping, freezing – now with all the hard work done they are afraid to cook it.

I get it. Wild game is sacred to me. The fear of error is normal; one should be respectful of all meat – wild meat especially.

This book will help alleviate that fear of wild game meat.

How? In the following chapters, I combine a lifelong love of hunting and a career's worth of professional cooking. The book provides simple recipes for common and exotic wild game – from snails to venison. My recipes aren't stuffy, requiring visits to gourmet food stores and expensive ingredients. I wrote these recipes for people who want to eat wild game as a part of a lifestyle, not as a part of a labored experience.

Need instruction on how to break down a deer? Check. Need a recipe for that uncle who hates goose meat? Got one. Want to impress a date with a fancy quail dinner? No problem. Found a pond with giant bullfrogs and want a lesson on hunting and cooking them? You have the right book in your hands.

While this book is far from exhaustive, it shows the diversity of game available and how best to eat it. Let me show you how I hunt, how I live, and how I cook. Let me share with you what it means to be a *Chef in the Wild.*

— Randy King

AIR

We set the decoys

and then we waited.

And waited. Finally, one lone honker

appeared on the horizon.

Someone laid on the call.

The goose swung our direction, circled a few times and then locked its wings to land among the decoys.

1

LESSONS FROM A GOOSE BLIND

The first time I sat in a goose blind I was eleven-years-old. It was a frozen January morning in a cut cornfield outside of Greenleaf. We had set out a flock of hollow plastic geese decoys while it was still dark. The goal was to trick the geese into thinking they could land in the decoys and be safe. Little did they know.

We set the decoys and then we waited. And waited. Finally, one lone honker appeared on the horizon. Someone laid on the call. The goose swung our direction, circled a few times and then locked its wings to land among the decoys. As soon as the goose was in range Dad whispered "take'em" in my ear. I pulled up and blasted. One shot and then another out of my 16 gauge side by side shotgun. The goose fell hard and fast to the ground.

I was shaking when I ran out to grab the bird but not from cold; the cold had gone away. The boredom of sitting endlessly was gone. All I could feel was a connection to something in my gut. It was like my inner cave boy was clawing its way out.

That was the only goose to come in that day. Four grown men and a child had spent the better part of a cold morning "hunting" geese with little luck. Yet no one seemed disappointed, everyone was happy, patting me on the back. It was a lesson in patience, mortality, kindness and support for a younger generation.

I never will forget my experience in the goose blind that day. But I know that I am not alone in having those experiences.

"Hunting is hardwired into the human psyche."

Dr. James Swan, Snow Goose Productions, author of In Defense of Hunting

Every now and then you get a book that just makes you want to wax philosophically about a subject. Well, at least I do. In downtown Nampa, I found a great little book called *In Defense of Hunting* by James Swan. From the title alone, it seemed like a book I could get behind. As it turns out Swan dedicated a whole lot of his book to his "spirit animal," the snow goose.

"The hunt has been with us for thousands of years. Hunting is firmly hardwired into the human psyche; an instinct for survival fueled by passion and guided by ethics that locks mankind into a kinship with nature. Honoring the hunting instinct, getting your hands bloody and dirty to put food on the table, naturally inspires one to know what thanksgiving really means."

Yeah, what he said.

"In life it is not what you know, it is who you know."

Drew Allen, Peppershock Media, Goose Hunter

"I've been goose hunting off and on since I was a kid. I remember getting up early with Dad, heading over to Grandma and Grandpa's to meet up with Grandpa and his buddies. Grandma had the coffee and doughnuts ready. We'd drive one mile down the road, set up in a field right off 12th Avenue and Locust Lane in Nampa and slay geese…Those days are long gone…. Basically it's become a "who you know" sport. I have a neighbor that would love to go more often, but he doesn't know where to go.

Don't get me wrong though...I still love getting up early, brewin' coffee and freezing my ass off even if we just end up watching a nice sunrise and bullshittin' the whole time."

"Things are not always as they appear."

Brannon Hancock, Counter Guy at Sportsman's Warehouse

Hunters fund wildlife conservation. Sounds a little counter intuitive but it's true. In 1937, the US government passed the Pittman-Robertson Act imposing an excise tax of 11% on all consumptive sporting goods. Consumptive goods are things like guns and bullets. That means that every $20 box shells steel shells I buy contributes $2.20 to the conservation of wildlife. If I was a better shot, my conservation dollars would actually decrease.

Having seen the lines at the sporting good stores this past Christmas season I know that a lot of money is going towards the sporting goods tax. Brannon Hancock had this to say about the Pittman-Robertson Act, "Speaking only for myself, I think it is marvelous. A great program. If we, hunters, don't have the resources (game) then companies lose a customer base…the cost is hidden in the item that is purchased."

"You are probably not the first person to have the idea."

Dr. Chris Hill, Professor of Anthropology, Boise State University

I called Dr. Hill in his office during finals week at BSU and he was kind enough to answer the phone. At first Dr. Hill was at a loss as to how he could help me, normally when he digs up bird bones for work they are not typically identified by species. However, he did mention a discovery in the dry caves of Nevada, "One of the most amazing discoveries is from Lovelock Cave in Nevada, where duck decoys have been found that are about 2,000 years old, probably slightly older." It just goes to show that hunters and decoys have a long standing relationship. While it is great to think you are original, you are unlikely to be the first one to have an idea.

"Don't sweat the details."

Jeff Rhodes, Owner, Winglocker Decoys

Sometimes it is just as effective to get the gist of a situation and react in real time as it is to be overly focused on the small things prior to the situation. This is often the case with goose hunting. Goose decoys are normally made with a high attention to detail. The heads are painted just so, everything is as close to lifelike as possible. But sometimes that is not the point at all.

"Look," said Jeff over the phone, "if a goose can see all the little details of your decoy then the darn thing should have already been shot." Jeff should know, he makes decoys. Not the normal, expensive ones but a silhouette decoy made out of cloth and wire. His decoys run about $36 per dozen while the high-end, very detailed decoys run about $400 per dozen. "What sells decoys is shelf appearance," Jeff added, "take a look at the expensive decoy at about 35 yards and tell me if all that detail matters."

I did, it doesn't. You don't always need to sweat the details.

Goose hunting is a metaphor for life. Important lessons are learned when you step outside your normal day-to-day events.

2

GAME ON

The cackle of a rooster sounds off to the left; you pivot, shoot and watch as the bird crumples into a tangle of brush. A few seconds later your dog, or your bird-dogging buddy, drops the dead pheasant at your feet. Dinner is secured for the night. What do you do with it now?

As a chef, I am frequently asked the best method for cooking game. The first rule of thumb it is to get it cool. The holes from your pellets are perfect avenues for bacteria and viruses to spread throughout the animal; from the outside in and the inside out. The body temperature that pheasants operate on is approximately the same as the optimal bacteria growth temperature. Stop bug growth: cool the birds as soon as possible.

Some argue that aging a bird is paramount to getting the most flavor. I am a little up in the air on this. I will age a bird if the conditions are right meaning no shot in the main body and it was cooled right away. I age my birds for just a few days: two to three for a pheasant, one to two for quail; however, if the rooster took a long ride in the truck at 70°F I will remove the innards and freeze or eat the bird right away.

The easiest way to remove the innards of a pheasant is with a small pair of game scissors. I peel back the feathers at the bottom of the breastbone and make a 1-inch long snip. Then I carefully cut under the skin without puncturing the intestines, along the breast to the backbone. The intestines will simply fall out of the bird. I snip the intestines as close to the rectum as possible and then cut the esophagus. Next I will insert the tip of one of the scissors blades into the rectum cavity and cut the bones. This allows me to remove the rest of the intestines and rinse the area with water.

When back at home I cut the head off the bird, leaving as much of the neck as I can, and remove the skin from the bird. I do not keep the skin on a pheasant because I generally utilize two cooking methods – one for the breast and one for the legs. I'll only leave the skin on a bird when it can be roasted whole. If you're going to roast a pheasant, you have to pluck it, and plucking a pheasant is an egregious event that I am not willing to participate in.

When the skinned bird is on the counter, I breast it out and leave the remaining meat on the carcass. The legs, back and neck meat are best when stewed or tossed into a slow cooker for several hours. The legs especially have many tendons that make eating them tricky unless they are cooked to fall-off-the-bone-tender. The neck and remaining bones will give off a large amount of gelatin and that makes for great soup and stew bases.

To breast a pheasant it is best to remove the wishbone first. In the gap between the neck and the breast I make small cuts with a boning knife until the wishbone can be removed with as little damage to the breast meat as possible. Then, using a sharp knife, I cut down the one side of the keel of the bird. The keel is the central, protruding section of the breastplate. The knife blade will slide easily through the meat and come to a rest on the rib bones. Then I turn the knife under the meat and slowly peel the breast away from the bones.

Pheasant is a white meat game bird and must be cooked to well done; it must reach an internal temperature of 165°F to be considered safe to eat.

When cooking pheasant, I treat it like chicken – it can be kind of bland and dries out easily. To remedy this I often add crusts or sauces to the breast to keep it moist. A good rule of thumb with wild game is to add what it lacks – most wild game lacks fat so fat (bacon and cream are two of my favorites) is often needed in the recipe.

Tortilla Chip Crusted Pheasant Breast with Hunters Style Corn Cakes

Serves 4

Slow Cooker Pheasant

You can save the broth created by the pheasant and use that in soups or stews if you wish.

1 pheasant, breasts removed
2 heads garlic
1 apple, quartered and seeded
1 small red onion, quartered
3 bay leaves
1 teaspoon cinnamon

Turn the slow cooker on low and add the pheasant and remaining ingredients. Add enough water to just cover the bird. Place the lid on the slow cooker and cook for 8-10 hours on low heat. Turn off and let rest for 1 hour. Remove bird, cool and pick meat from the carcass. Reserve.

Hunters Style Corn Cakes

1 box instant cornbread mix, Jiffy or equivalent
¾ cup canned black beans, rinsed and drained
Slow cooker pheasant meat
1 teaspoon red chili flakes
2 eggs
Milk
2 tablespoons honey
Salt and freshly ground pepper

Preheat oven to "warm."

Mix the beans, pheasant meat, chili flakes, eggs, and honey together in a medium-sized bowl. Add the cornbread mix to the bowl and mix. Add milk as needed to thin the batter to a pancake-batter-like consistency. Salt and pepper to taste.

Heat a large sauté pan on medium-low heat for 4 minutes. The pan must be warm or the corn cakes will stick. Lightly coat the bottom of the pan with spray oil and pour ¼ cup cakes. Make sure to leave enough room between them so they do not touch. Cook cakes until golden brown on one side, 2-3 minutes, and flip and brown the other side. Reserve the corn cakes in a warm oven.

Tortilla Chip Crusted Pheasant Breast

2 pheasant breasts
1 cup crushed corn tortilla chips
¼ cup flour
¼ cup milk
Salt and freshly ground pepper
¼ cup canola oil

Preheat oven to 400°F.

The easiest and cleanest way to make this recipe is with 3 one-gallon zip-seal baggies: put the flour, milk and crushed chips each in their own bag. Then place the pheasant breasts in the flour bag and shake. Transfer to the milk bag and shake. Transfer breasts over to the chip bag and shake. Make sure to press the breasts with chips so that they stick well.

Heat canola oil over medium heat in a medium sauté pan. Cook breasts to golden brown, then flip. Transfer the whole pan into the oven and bake for 7-10 minutes or until the pheasant breast reaches 155°F. Remove from oven and cover. The bird will cook itself, from residual heat, to 165°F.

Serve each pheasant breast with 2 corn cakes.

3

TURKEY: NEVER AS PLANNED

The gobbler was on the top of a small finger draw strutting his stuff when I caught sight of him in my binoculars. He was not overly large, not a jake, but a respectable Merriam's turkey.

I was in the high country just outside of Riggins experiencing a frustrating weekend of turkey chasing. I could get the toms to gobble but then they'd run in the opposite direction of my call. Eventually, I ditched my "tried and true" techniques: I stopped setting up, stopped calling, and stopped hooting like an owl. Now, I was spot and stalk turkey hunting and I was doing it with my longbow.

I had a clear view of the mountainside from the top of a ridge. The birds had congregated on a specific section made up of three finger draws and a mountainside that was edged by canyons. It was on the top of one of those fingers I found my long beard.

The trees fell quiet as I slipped into them – the squirrels shut up, the birds stopped chirping. It was like all the living things in the woods were trying to rat me out to the turkey. I held my breath and closed the distance. I watched as the bird crested and then dropped into a draw. He was heading down the hill to thick cover. I bolted.

I ditched the decoys, the binoculars, my camo coat – I ran as fast as I could. My plan was to crest ahead of the gobbler, let him close the distance to me, and then stick him from behind a tree.

My plan was working perfectly. I came in ahead of the bird. I could see him walking on a game trail, if he stayed on course he would be directly downhill from my location. Absolutely perfect, I nocked an arrow and reminded myself to breathe.

The tom stayed on the trail and was in near ideal placement when I drew my bow back to shoot. I had the form down. I knew the distance. I could feel the shot, and I was notching the tag in my brain. As the bird was walking down the path, I was tracking him with my bow. I figured in my lead for the shot and let the arrow fly.

And then I remembered something my father had told me, "Boy," he said, "if a turkey could smell, you'd never shoot one. They can't see very well, but it is that damn ability to hear that keeps them safe."

My shot was a good one, but out of the corner of my eye I watched as the bird stopped dead in its tracks when he heard the sound of my string. The dull "plunk" of my 55-pound longbow string was a noise that was out of place in these woods. I was busted. My lead was 6 inches too far in front of the gobbler. I watched in agony as the tip of my broad head fluffed the swaying beard of the tom. He took three steps and was soaring to the bottom of the canyon. It was a long walk back to camp.

The next morning I climbed a ridgeline the turkeys frequented. When I crested I saw two jakes strutting in the sun. I clicked the safety off my 12 gauge and paralleled one of them. Finally.

I wish I could cook a wild turkey like a Butterball. But, alas, the two birds are not even close to the same thing. Wild turkeys actually use their muscle, which makes them tough meat; sometimes the legs are downright inedible. To alleviate the problem of tough legs, especially drumsticks, I section the bird out. I remove the breasts, then the whole leg. Then I break down the leg at the joint into two sections: the thigh and the drumstick. The thigh meat can be a little tough, but it is nothing compared to the drumsticks.

Like Butterball drumsticks, wild gobblers tend to have large boney sections of tendon that pass through the leg meat. I remove these by running my knife blade around the top of the drumstick to cut the tendons loose. Then I run my blade right along the bone about a third of the way down the drumstick. This exposes most of the tendons. Next, using a multi-tool or a clean set of pliers, I start yanking out as many of the tendons as possible, cutting out any that remain.

After the tendons are gone most of the bone will be exposed, and it will look like a big bulb of meat is attached to the end. I like to cook wild turkey drumsticks like a lamb shank or osso buco, long and slow to dissolve the connective tissue and make the meat tender.

Curried Wild Turkey Drumsticks

Serves 2

2 cleaned wild turkey or domestic turkey drumsticks
1 onion, chopped
1 red pepper, chopped
2 tablespoons butter
2 tablespoons red curry paste
12 oz. can coconut milk, sweet is fine
1 cup chicken stock or water
1 tablespoon yellow curry powder
1 tablespoon chopped garlic
1 lime, cut in half
Salt and freshly ground pepper

Melt butter over medium heat in a medium-sized sauté pan. Brown the drumsticks in the butter on each side for 3-4 minutes.

Add the onion and red pepper and sauté for 2 more minutes. Mix the curry paste, coconut milk, curry powder, garlic, chicken stock and lime in a small bowl until blended; pour over the turkey legs. Bring the pan to a simmer and cover. Let simmer over low heat (or in 250°F oven) for 3 hours.

Remove the drumsticks from the pan and place on a bed of white rice. Then reduce the remaining juices in the pan until slightly thickened. Serve over wild turkey drumsticks.

Breaded Turkey Cutlets with Oil Poached Garlic and Tomatoes served with Pan Roasted Orange

This recipe calls for turkey "cutlets" which are just slices of turkey breast. Lay your breast out on the counter. It will make half of a heart shape. Cut across the grain of the meat in ¼ inch sections. You will get quite a few. It is even a little easier to cut when the meat is frozen a little. Take those slices and place them between two sheets of clear plastic film about an inch from each other. Use a mallet or the bottom of a pan to hammer the slices into almost see through thin sections. You now have turkey "cutlets." Bread them and fry them, add a squeeze of lemon, and you have the German classic schnitzel. Replace the lemon with a sweeter caramelized orange and add the roasted garlic and tomatoes – bang – a whole new take on a classic.

Serves 2

Oil Poached Garlic and Tomatoes

1 cup olive oil
1 cup garlic cloves, peeled
1 cup cherry or grape tomatoes

Place the garlic, tomatoes and oil in a small sauce pan. Turn heat to medium low and let simmer for 20 minutes. Reserve in a warm location. This will create more than you need for this recipe. Store in a mason jar in the fridge, covered in oil and it will last up to a year. Just microwave the jar when you want some roasted garlic and tomatoes.

Pan Roasted Orange

2 oranges, cut in half
1 tablespoon canola oil
Heat oil in a medium-sized cast iron skillet. Place orange halves, flesh side down in the pan and heat on medium until the exposed orange flesh is dark brown. Remove pan from heat. Reserve.

Turkey Cutlets

8 2 oz. turkey cutlets
1 cup flour
1 cup milk
2 cups bread crumbs
1 tablespoon freshly ground pepper
1 tablespoon salt
1 tablespoon Italian seasoning herb blend
¼ cup canola oil

Heat canola oil in a large sauté pan or cast iron on medium heat until a wooden spoon inserted into the oil gives off bubbles and floats. (This is an old German trick that I learned in Singapore, long story…all I know is that it works. The oil temperature will be about 350°F).

Gather three small bowls. Place the flour, milk and bread crumbs in separate bowls. In the flour bowl add the pepper, Italian seasoning and salt. Mix.

Place cutlets in the flour and coat all sides evenly. Then place the cutlet in the milk, wetting all sides. Place the cutlet in the bread crumbs, forcefully pushing bread crumbs onto all parts of the turkey cutlet. Reserve the breaded cutlet on a plate. Bread the remaining slices.

Carefully place one cutlet at a time in the hot oil. Cook the cutlet until it is "GB&D," or golden brown and delicious on one side, then flip. Cook the other side until GB&D as well. Reserve the fried cutlets on a paper towel lined plate.

Place two cutlets on a plate and top with a mix of oil poached garlic and tomatoes. Take one half of an orange and squeeze on top of the breaded turkey.

4

SAGE, SAGE GROUSE

When the manila envelope arrived in the mail from Idaho Fish and Game, I was concerned. Never before had I received such a large package from a government agency. Most of the time my mail from the IDFG is a survey or a "you forgot to file your harvest report" notice. Inside was a note asking me to send in the wings of the sage grouse that I was planning on shooting.

The package had prepaid postage, wax envelopes and a letter telling me about the importance of data collection. The letter even had specific directions on what part of the wing that the IDFG wanted: "try to send us the wing with the fewest shot off, blood stained, dog chewed and otherwise damaged feathers." Got it.

It felt dirty, a little wrong, to package up a dead upland game animals' wings and send through the mail. But if it was what I had to do in order to hunt the birds I was going to comply.

Hunting sage grouse is not a guaranteed thing. They are in a difficult position around much of the country. A few hundred years ago, before roads and subdivisions divided the landscape, a lot of the West was unaltered tracts of sage brush. These large areas allowed sage hen to roam freely and maintain healthy population levels. But with the encroachment of man and the consequent habitat change, some areas have seen a population loss of sage grouse of up to 80%. According to the Nature Conservancy website, if left to the status quo, the sage grouse population is expected to decline by another 19% in the Intermountain West.

Populations of sage grouse have diminished to the point that hunting them has been limited to a single week most years. Some years, in times of drought or very cold and wet springs, the season has been canceled all together. Other years, due to fire, certain areas cannot be hunted. Each year the Idaho Fish and Game decides when and where the birds can be harvested and the hunting season information often doesn't come out until a month before the season starts. For a native bird that has been hunted for hundreds of years by Idaho's inhabitants not having a season is hard to swallow.

Compare the short season of sage grouse to other game birds. Quail, for example, have a four and a half-month-long season. You can hunt them from September to January.

Idaho has a plan to keep the hunting and the conservation of sage grouse a priority. Idaho Fish and Game, the Nature Conservancy and several other agencies and non-profits have banded together to help protect and restore sage grouse habitat.

I spoke with Ken Miracle, of the Idaho Nature Conservancy, about what they are doing to help the sage grouse population. "What we do is go in and remove the junipers that have encroached on the wetland habitat. With the over fighting of fires, junipers have started to thrive in non-traditional areas like meadows…when they show up meadows tend to dry up and go away, junipers can absorb a lot of water."

To remove the junipers, the group uses a tree chipper. "What we do is called mastication, we mulch and spread the juniper over the whole area. This is a lot better than just felling the tree and letting it lie since that provides obstacles for cows, elk and deer."

The removal of junipers has a secondary benefit of getting rid of hawk roosts and other sage grouse predators. Most of the work the nature conservancy does is on private land, since most of the water is on private ground.

As a human predator I am amazed at the sage grouse, *Centrocercus urophasianus.* They belong, roughly, to the same family as the chicken. Hence, I think, their nicknames – sage hen and prairie chicken. The birds do elaborate mating dances – puffing up their chests and making a bleating noise that can be heard for hundreds of yards. They sound like a helicopter when spooked from underneath some scrub. What the big birds lack in coordination and maybe even tact, they make up for in size. They are, on average, about twice the size of the other grouse in Idaho: mature toms (male birds), can be the size of a small turkey.

I know of a few wetland areas, called "stands" by my IDFG contacts, that hold sage grouse. If all goes well opening day, I will be taking my oldest boy out to harvest his first sage grouse. We will be high up in the Owyhee Mountains, replicating a hunt that five generations of my family have participated in.

After having hunted sage grouse for a few years, wandering the high desert slopes, I have learned something about myself. Sage hen offer a dilemma – I hunt them. I kill them and then eat them. But they taste like crap. It seems that no amout of Cajun seasoning can cover up their resemblance to overcooked liver. Eating them is a chore: it's the responsible thing to do, but not the joy that eating other wild game can be.

I hunt them anyway. I want the predator-prey relationship on what I consider my home turf; I want to use my incisor teeth, my tools and my brain. I like to hunt the birds; I just wish they tasted better.

Ken Miracle does not share the same opinion of the birds. "Sometimes I hunt the sage grouse for meat…I like the big old toms. Shooting them has less of an impact on the population and they make excellent chili."

I think I need to get his recipe. I will continue to hunt sage hen each year, one per day. Because I can. Because I want to. Because I am not sure how much longer I will be able to. And I will make sure to send in my wings with the fewest shot-off, blood-stained, dog-chewed and otherwise damaged feathers.

Sage Grouse and Black Bean Chili

As anyone who has ever made ground beef tacos knows, it is almost impossible to get ground meat properly browned. With most meats, the common practice is grind the meat, then brown. NO! Brown the meat then grind it for the best flavor and to avoid a water-logged pan of boiled meat. If you are not in the mood for grinding, brown the meat and then hand dice when cool. Browning meat adds great flavor and depth to a dish.

Serves 8

2 tablespoons butter
1 sage grouse, deboned

Cut grouse meat into sections, about 1 inch by 1 inch. Heat cast iron skillet or Dutch oven on medium heat. Add butter. When butter is melted but not brown add half the meat. Brown on all sides. Remove meat to plate and put remaining meat in pan. Repeat browning with remaining meat. Rough chop or grind all meat and reserve.

1 large yellow onion, diced
10 cloves garlic, crushed
1 red bell pepper, seeded and diced
1 Anaheim pepper, seeded and diced
1 jalapeño pepper, seeded and diced
1 28 oz. can diced tomatoes
1 8 oz. can tomato sauce
1 12 oz. can cheap light beer
4 juniper berries
2 12 oz. cans black beans, drained and rinsed
1 tablespoon cocoa powder
2 tablespoons chili powder
2 tablespoons cumin
1½ tablespoons oregano
1 tablespoon sugar
1 teaspoon apple cider vinegar
Salt and freshly ground pepper, to taste

In the same pan that the meat was browned in, add the diced yellow onion and crushed garlic. Cook on medium heat for 5 minutes or until the onion begins to turn translucent. Next add the bell pepper, Anaheim and jalapeño to the pot. Cook for 2-3 minutes, until fragrant. Add the diced tomatoes, tomato sauce, beer and juniper berries.

Bring mixture to a simmer and add the sage grouse to the pan. Simmer covered for 2 hours, stirring occasionally.

When meat is tender add the black beans, cocoa powder, chili powder, cumin, oregano, sugar and apple cider vinegar to the pan. Stir and simmer for 20 minutes to let the flavors develop. Season with salt and pepper as needed.

Serve hot and garnish with cilantro, shredded cheddar cheese, Fritos and chopped green onions.

5

THE SOMEDAY GOOSE

I listened closely for my cue to spring into action. Above me, hundreds of ducks seemed to be falling out of the sky onto our decoy spread. "Wait for it," my buddy whispered to me. A mallard hen walked past my head and a few geese looked on from 100 yards up, skeptical.

We had set up our decoys in a tilled-under cornfield. The Reams brothers, Leon and Mike, had been nice enough to dig four coffin-style blinds. I lay in the blind and waited for the brothers to call in the waterfowl. When the ducks got within 30 yards, Leon cried, "Take'em!" and we all sat up and shot.

In one hour, we had shot our duck limit: 21. The only problem was the distinct lack of goose commitment.

Weeks later, I was sitting in a lawn chair in shin-deep ice water on the Snake River waiting for geese to lock wings onto our decoy spread. I would watch them from the cover of the blind circle and circle and circle before finally flaring off. That day, I shot a goldeneye and a few mallards. Again, I could not get a goose to commit. Flocks would look down on us and then head to the city parks.

Back in a cornfield; one dead pigeon, no geese. Winter wheat field, no geese. Finally, desperation set in. I went to the Boise River and put on a big sneak.

My dog and I belly crawled to the edge of the river, sneaking a peek on a flock. They liked a particular back eddy, especially when it was cold and nasty. Then the dog and I waited for shooting light, shivering in the reeds trying to stay quiet.

I blame the dog for what happened next – she gets a little hyper when her job is coming up. It was time: I rose and crept closer to the edge of the water. But, mid-sneak, she bolted 30 yards in front of me. All hell broke loose – over a hundred geese rose off the water in a matter of seconds. Spook and shoot goose hunting! I ran as fast as my legs in 10-ply camo waders could take me to the edge of the water and busted a goose back into the river.

We all have that friend that is a little slower at sensing social cues, the one who is late to their own birthday party. That is the goose I shot, the last one off the water. The last one to figure out that something was wrong and it needed to fly. I kind of regret taking the slow one out of the gene pool because geese are smart enough as it is.

The dog retrieved the goose and all was right with the world. That is until she, the dog, shook off the excess water on her fur. Well, she tried to shake it off but the water was frozen in spikes along her spine. She started running in circles to stay warm. Ridgebacks aren't water dogs, especially not cold water dogs, so we hustled back to the truck and I put her in the front seat, heater on high, wrapped in a towel. She now expects this kind of treatment, I am afraid.

It was time to start cooking.

Making something out of goose that my children crave is my criterion for success. If I can take an animal and get it in the bellies of my three boys, I have won. That said, I often turn to their favorite food for inspiration – Chinese take-out. The boys are General Tso fans, orange chicken freaks and lovers of cashew chicken. So, I make duck and goose in those preparations. Even more delicious is a Peking duck with crispy skin and hoisin sauce.

Unfortunately, the Peking process is a pain in the butt. It involves an air compressor, marinating, poaching, fan-drying and then roasting. But I love the flavor so much I crave it.

So this is my compromise recipe: a faux Peking duck (in this case, goose) without the hassle. Keep the flavor; lose the pain in the tushy prep.

Sesame Fried Goose with Allspice Pancakes and Hoisin Sauce

Serves 4

Velveting Batter

2 cups canola oil
1 frozen goose breast, skinless, slightly thawed
¼ cup + 1 tablespoon corn starch
2 eggs, separated
1 tablespoon black sesame seeds
1 teaspoon freshly ground pepper

Pancakes

1 cup corn muffin mix, Jiffy or equivalent
1 cup pancake batter
1 tablespoon allspice
Water

Garnish

¼ cup thinly sliced red pepper
1 green onion
¼ cup hoisin sauce, heated through

In a medium-sized bowl blend corn muffin mix, pancake batter and allspice. Add water until a thin batter is formed. Heat a large non-stick skillet over medium-high heat. Pour ⅛-cup-sized pancakes, brown both sides. Keep warm. Yield: approximately 15 pancakes.

Cut goose into thin strips, a little more than a ¼-inch wide, against the grain. Keep mostly frozen until it is time to cut because most meat is easier to cut when slightly frozen, especially into strips.

In a clean metal bowl whip the eggs until a thick white foam forms. Add in sesame seeds and pepper. Whip a little more. Slowly add the corn starch and stir gently. A batter the consistency of cream will form.

Toss the sliced goose in remaining 1 tablespoon corn starch. Dredge meat in batter. Heat oil to 350°F in a large heavy pan or Dutch oven. Cook goose in hot oil until golden brown and delicious.

Toss with hot hoisin sauce, red peppers and green onion. Serve with cornmeal pancakes.

6

ARMCHAIR QUAIL HUNTERS

The other boat on the water had been playing hopscotch with us all day. My buddy Ryan and I would pull onto a small riparian bar along the Snake River to hunt quail; they would motor past hooting and hollering at us. The boaters seemed to be more intent on the 12 ounce beer curl and being our peanut gallery than doing any hunting. They never fired one shot, but they offered us our own private hunting heckling section.

It never failed that they would motor to within shouting distance when a covey of quail would bust up. The boaters would offer shooting suggestions to us while we fired away at the birds. Comments like "Oh! Just missed!" and "A little behind that one!" came off the water, unwelcome. They thought they were being hysterical. We did not.

It occurred to me later that this was a classic case of armchair quail hunting. Offer advice on how to shoot a quail, while not actually shooting at the birds. Most hunters I know, myself included, are fantastic at this. We can tell others, all day long, the proper technique, lead time and choke to use for hunting the little birds. That said, in the field, most of armchair quailers can't hit one in five birds.

Over time I have noticed that armchair quail hunters tend to have a rash of equipment issues when out hunting. The gun's action isn't working right. The safety is sticking. The wrong choke is in the gun. Creative reasons de jour escape every honest quail hunter's mouth. As well as some profanities when a shot is missed.

It seems that the birds also have a great sense of timing. Hopping the fence? Time to bust up. Taking a pee? Never fails, birds will fly.

This combination of poor shooting, equipment "failure" and the birds' knack for timing makes every precious ounce of quail meat all the more valuable. A hunter can spend an entire day out and get four birds with pride. Which it turns out isn't even enough of an appetizer for his family. Hitting a flying quail is hard, plain and simple. They humble me.

Over the years, I have picked up a few tricks for getting quail into my vest. The first thing I recommend is learn to whistle like a quail, or buy a quail call. When a covey busts, they will start calling out to each other in hopes of connecting and relocating. Give a busted covey a few minutes and then hit the call. They will reply – alerting you to the location of a few more birds hiding in the rough.

After busting the covey, it is a good idea to stop and mark the location they flew to. Then take a five minute break. If you immediately follow the birds, they will tend to run and disappear. If you give them a little time to settle they will be more likely to bust again giving hunters a good shot opportunity.

The single biggest factor for quail success is a dog. I don't care if it is a Yorkie with ear plugs, just about any dog when hunting quail is better than no dog. That said the dog has to stay close to be effective. While a nice pointer would be invaluable, any mutt with its nose to the ground and the drive to make birds fly will prove effective.

We did not reach our limit on the river that day. But we did show ourselves the limit of our shooting capabilities. I realized I needed to bust more clay in the off-season and that I needed to check what choke I had in my gun.

One day I will be able to limit out on quail. The perfect shooter somewhere inside me will present itself and I will manage to whack ten in one day. I'll take that limit home and actually be able to make a whole meal for my family; like my buddy and fellow quail hunter Matt Lindley says, "You need to walk a lot and shoot a lot just to get a little stew."

Smashed Quail with Mountain Dew Ponzu

Like many people of my generation Mountain Dew was a food group when we were growing up. Over the years I've tried to turn this beverage into various things including desserts, corn cakes and in this case, a sauce for quail. The drink has two major flavors in it – citrus and sugar. A classic Asian-style ponzu sauce has three flavors – citrus, sugar and soy. Use the Mountain Dew as a base and you are ⅔ the way to a ponzu sauce.

Serves 4

8 quail, plucked and gutted
1 can Mountain Dew
½ cup soy sauce
1 teaspoon red chili flakes
2 green onions, sliced
1 thumb-sized chunk of ginger, peeled and sliced

To "smash" the quail all that you need to do is lay them on their backs, breast up, and press firmly down with your hand. This will crush the ribs and flatten out the bird allowing for more even cooking. Another option for a "smashed quail" is to cut the back and ribs out of the bird with a pair of kitchen scissors. Place the bird breast side down on the cutting board. With the scissors cut between the legs and then remove the rib cage with two additional cuts. The cutting will look like a "Y." Without the backbone the bird will cook more quickly and evenly.

Place sauce ingredients in a small pan. Bring to a simmer over medium-high heat and cook for 10 minutes. Chill. Marinate the quail overnight in the Mountain Dew sauce.

Preheat grill to medium. Grill marinated quail pouring small amounts of the sauce over the top while it cooks. Be careful not to burn: the sauce has high sugar content and will burn easily. Grill and repeat sauce treatment until a firm crust forms.

Soba Noodle Salad

You can use any kind of round noodle for this recipe. I have used angel hair and spaghetti in the past. Soba noodles are just a Japanese take on the thin round noodle made from buckwheat. You can find them dry or fresh in most grocery stores. Look in the ethnic section for the dry noodles and in produce for the fresh.

12 oz. cooked and chilled soba noodles
1 lime, juice and zest
1 red pepper, thinly sliced
½ red onion, thinly sliced
2 tablespoons soy sauce
1 tablespoon sesame seeds
2 green onions, thinly sliced
Salt and freshly ground pepper

Mix lime juice, pepper, onion, soy sauce, and sesame seeds until well blended. Toss noodles, lime mixture, and lime zest with the noodles in a medium-sized bowl. Salt and pepper to taste.

Place the noodles in the center of a plate. Pour a small amount of Mountain Dew ponzu around the noodles. Top with hot quail. Serve.

7

LOATHSOME DOVE

Uncle Dave's ranch borders Jump Creek near Homedale. The property has a nice tree-lined section of creek bottom and the agricultural land provides ample seeds and sustenance for all sorts of game animals. It is perfect bird hunting country; I have seen pheasant, quail, duck, geese, and a host of other avian creatures. Unfortunately, it has been invaded by foreigners – beady-eyed genetic giants have taken over sections of his property. Well, more like they flutter around and eat some of his corn.

The invaders are Eurasian collared doves and they are found across the US and are quickly migrating to Canada as well. Originally from, as their name implies, Asia and Europe, they have been on the invasive path for most of the last century. They conquered Western Europe by the 1950s, the Bahamas by 1970 and can now found all the way to the southern border of Alaska.

The story goes that Eurasian collared doves were accidentally released during a burglary at a pet store on an island in the Bahamas. A hurricane then transported them to Florida. According to Sal Palazzolo of Idaho Fish and Game: "They have steadily been spreading across the country since."

Eurasian collared doves resemble the American mourning dove in many ways. A dove is a dove is a dove. But upon closer inspection a collared dove has a black ring of feathers around its neck, it is often lighter in color and has a squared off tail. On average ECD are also bigger than mourning doves.

I'm interested in ECD's because I'm a hunter and in Idaho it's always open season for collared doves; you can bag as many as you want, any day of the year. All Fish and Game asks is that the hunter leave an identifiable portion of the bird intact, otherwise it will count toward your mourning dove limit. If hunting ECD's in the off-season, they will slap you with a poaching ticket if they can't ID the bird; mourning doves are a federally protected species.

I spoke with Jackson Landers, author of *Eating Aliens*, about the best way to hunt ECD's. "Hunting collared doves should be one part of our eradication efforts. It won't be the whole answer, but it should be part of it. Wing-shooters will need to spend time watching both collared doves and mourning doves in flight before going hunting, especially when the mourning dove is not in season. Their flight behavior is different and with practice a hunter can learn to tell the difference instantly in mid-air. Without practice, you might shoot the wrong species and earn yourself a fine from the game warden."

In *Eating Aliens* Jackson scours the country for invasive species and then eats them. The opening chapter features giant iguanas in Florida and the book closes with hunting pigs in Texas. It is a great read on just how much change an invasive species can cause in a given environment and why, as a society, we need to better manage our environments. Landers believes hunting (and then eating), can help with the eradication of invasive species.

Personally, I hunt ECD's because it gives me another game animal to eat. Without a bag limit I have the potential to score a couple grass-fed, organic, free-range, hormone free dinners in the off-season But I am a little less ethical with the ECD's than I am with other game birds. Most hunters let the birds fly and shoot them on the "wing." This increases the birds chance of survival and is considered more sporting than shooting them while they are sitting on a branch. I'll shoot an ECD while it's sitting on a branch and not give it a second thought. Why? My goal is eradication.

Eating these doves is quite enjoyable. According to Landers, "In my experience, one species of dove or pigeon tastes pretty much like every other species. If you like to eat mourning doves (which I do), then you will enjoy eating collared doves. Expect a rich, tightly grained red meat that has more in common with goose or beef than with chicken." Yum.

While the ECD is not supposed to be here, neither are a lot of the things around us. Looking at the environment of the Treasure Valley, we can see a whole host of non-native species. Honey bees, earthworms, dandelions, cheat grass, bullfrogs, quail, pheasants, chukar, catfish, bass, crappie, bluegill, perch, walleye, German brown trout, Hungarian partridges, pigeons (just to name a few!) are all non-native species to Idaho. But no massive removal efforts are underway. In fact most of the animals on that list are managed to keep populations steady and harvestable through hunting.

In most cases introduced or invasive species are relegated to three categories. The first category is the "remove at all cost invasive species" – like the feral swine that were found near CJ Strike a few years back. The second is the "it would be cool if they were gone but we don't have the budget to fight them right now" category. Carp, bullfrogs and the Eurasian collared dove seem to be in this category. The last category is the "introduced invader". Wild turkeys are a great example of the introduced invader; they are non-native to this section of the country but can only be hunted specific times of the year, with strict bag limits and licensing.

"Invasive and introduced is a matter of semantics," says Palazzolo, "If we want them here they are introduced, if we don't, they are invasive."

Dove Pot Pie

Chicken pot pie was a staple in my house growing up. I wish I could tell the world that my family made them from scratch but, more often than not, they were of the frozen variety. Those little pies still hold a place in my heart, mostly because they taste really, really good. This is my version of pot pie – while it's not entirely from scratch, it's a little more sophisticated due to the dove and apples.

Serves 4

2 slices of bacon, sliced into thin strips
4 doves, cut into breasts, legs and with heart and liver
½ cup diced carrot
½ cup diced celery
1 cup diced onion
2 cloves of garlic, diced
2 Granny Smith apples (or other tart, firm, baking apple), diced
3 tablespoons all-purpose flour
1½ cups milk
½ cup apple juice
Salt and freshly ground pepper
Fresh sage
1 cup cheddar cheese, shredded or cut into slabs
Prepared piecrust

Preheat oven to 400°F.

In a medium-sized stockpot cook the bacon until crispy. Add the dove meat, the heart and the liver. When the meat is brown add the carrot, celery, onion, garlic and apple. Cook until the onion is translucent. Next add the flour and incorporate well. Add the milk and apple juice. Cook over medium heat until the mixture thickens slightly. Turn heat to low and thicken to desired consistency. Salt, pepper and fresh sage to taste.

Separate the mixture evenly into baking dishes. Top with cheese.

Bake until the crust is golden brown and the mixture inside is bubbling, about 20 minutes.

8

PEACHES AND CREAM GROUSE

One archery season when I was in high school, remarkably, my neighbors agreed to let me stay in their cabin near Stanley. They also let me borrow a 90cc dirt bike. I must have had someone fooled, but I took advantage of the situation.

I strapped my bow to the front of the 60's era dirt bike and set off on previously inaccessible areas and goat trails. I was a young hunter and didn't quite comprehend that the noise I was making was perhaps the reason I wasn't seeing any wild animals. After all, the grouse still hung around.

And man did I see a lot of those birds. Families of five or six running, then fluttering up into a pine tree at eye level. I had never shot one so I just left them alone. Back at the cabin that night I looked up grouse in the Idaho upland regulations. I could shoot two, and the season had opened the same day as my archery tag. Sweet.

The next morning I found the birds 50 yards from were they had been the night before. They seemed way too calm as I approached them, arrow on the nock.

I shot the first one with a blunt. Bad idea. The grouse was only about 20 feet away when I gave it hell from my 55# compound. The blunt went clear through the breast of the bird and both came tumbling out of the tree. I tried saving as much of the bird as I could but the breast meat was ruined.

The next grouse I shot was with a broad head, again, out of a tree. I am fairly sure that an archeologist will find an arrow is stuck in a tree in the Sawtooth National Forest that has my name on it. The bird, luckily, came sliding off the shaft of the arrow and tumbled to the ground. Yet again most of the breast meat was ruined.

Limited out on grouse, I went back to thinking a deer would be standing in the road just around the next corner. No such luck.

Back at the cabin I boiled up the grouse bits and had a nice snack. I vowed that I would figure out a non-wasteful manner of harvesting these birds with my bow. That…or just come back up with the dog and shotgun.

Tips for grouse hunting

If you're bow hunting, a good judo point works great on grounded and treed grouse. I carry a judo point on my bow during archery season that I mark with a special color so it's easier to identify. I would hate to have a judo point on the knock when sneaking up on a buck.

Good 6 shot is normally more than enough for a grouse. But sometimes they flush fast after some pressure. At that point I switch to a size 4 "long shot" on my 16 gauge. These seem to give me an extra 10 yards or so of range and that comes in handy putting birds down.

Turkey season is a great time to do some grouse scouting. In the spring the mating call of a grouse is a distinctive low-tuned thump. The males pick a location, often a fallen log, and make that their home base. They hang near this log all year round. If you hear the thumping in the spring remember the location, or better yet mark it as a waypoint on your GPS. The bird should be within a few hundred yards of where you heard him in the spring.

Young grouse are stupid; they are called "fool hens" for a reason. These birds make awesome practice for young bowhunters. As a kid I would tag along with my dad, bow in hand, just for a shot at a young grouse. I have even made bows and arrows and hunted the birds for more sport. Nothing says "mountain man" like coming out of the woods with a grouse and a self-made bow.

Flocks of sage hen tend to frequent the same areas year after year. They stay in "stands" and when you know the location keep it a secret. I have hunted the same bowl in Owyhee County for four years in a row. I limit out by 8 am most days.

Know your different types of grouse. Some areas have sharp-tail and sage hen, but only sharp-tail is in open season. Shooting the first prairie-chicken that takes off can lead to some tense moments if it's the wrong type of bird.

Know the coverage that holds birds. In tree-lined areas I tend to hunt the ridgelines with the buck brush. In heavy cover I tend to hunt the logging roads. Your area is different so take notes from year to year about where the birds live and where they don't.

Tips for cooking grouse

A grouse, aside from a sage hen, is just about the closest wild-game animal to a chicken that I can think of. As such, I treat the bird as if it was a chicken. First, I decapitate and then pluck the bird. Then I disembowel it, saving the heart and liver for a fireside snack.

Since grouse is white meat it will need to be cooked until it is well done (165 °F). This will kill just about any bug or parasite that the "fool hen" might have.

When cooking a grouse, just like a chicken, the recipes for the breast are always the easiest ones to come up with. Chicken Parmesan, chicken alfredo, chicken piccata are all great classic ways to eat the bird. The one problem with those recipes – what the heck to do with the rest of the grouse?

One preparation I particularly like is separating the "tenderloin" off of the breast meat and then using it as stuffing for the thigh meat. First I breast out the grouse. On the bottom side of the bird will be a little finger of meat that is no longer attached to the breast. This is the "tender" or the "strip" that has accompanied countless kids meals for the past fifty years. Remove the tender and set it aside.

Then, I take the legs and separate them out at the thigh/knee joint. With the tip of a sharp knife, I remove the equivalent of the femur bone from the thigh meat. Folding the tender onto itself I place the meat back where the femur came from. Using the skin and a thin slice of Prosciutto I wrap the whole package, placing it seam-side down to allow the natural moisture to form a seal.

Peaches and Cream Grouse Bundles

These little thigh/tender bundles are great for grilling. Bacon also works as a substitute for the Prosciutto though it can overpower the flavor of the grouse.

Serves 2

4 Prosciutto-wrapped grouse bundles (see previous page)
1 almost ripe peach
1 shallot, diced fine
1 tablespoon butter
¼ cup heavy whipping cream
1 tablespoon honey
Salt and freshly ground pepper
Fresh sprigs mint

Heat grill to medium high. Grill the grouse bundles until the juices run clear, about 3 minutes on each side.

Bring a small saucepan of water to a boil, just big enough to hold the peach. Cut an X on the bottom of the peach and, with a pair of tongs, submerge it into the boiling water and count to 20. Carefully remove peach and run under cold tap water for 1 minute. The skin should come right off. Core the peach and slice thinly.

Melt butter in a medium-sized sauté pan over medium-high heat, add the shallots and sauté them until almost browned. Add the peaches and the honey. Let cook for a few moments until the peaches begin to brown.

Add the cream and reduce the heat to low. Let simmer for 2-3 minutes or until the cream thickens. Salt and pepper to taste.

You can serve the grouse bundles whole or sliced with the sauce on the side for dipping. Delicious with Hattie's Mashers.

9

THE LUNCH BREAK CHUKAR

On the off chance that I get a lunch break, I like to take the opportunity to go chukar hunting. You see I work exactly nine minutes from a Wildlife Management Area on the southeast side of Boise. It isn't the least popular place to hunt in the world but I have never seen another hunter when I'm there, most likely because they are all at work.

Some have "working lunches" to feel productive. I have "hunting lunches" to increase my productivity. I come back to work refreshed and ready to conquer. The goal for me is to bag a bird, but honestly I don't care if I fire a single shot. I am out hunting to be away from work, escape the stress and maybe find dinner.

I pack a lunch and my trusty 16 gauge double and strike out with exactly 42 minutes of hunting time. I hike along a trail as far as I can for 15 minutes – the trails are very good so I can easily make progress. Then I'll "bushwhack" my way back to the truck with the remaining time.

Chukars don't frequent the bottom of the riparian areas like quail; they tend to be either on top of the rim rock or just below it. The nastier the terrain, the more likely it is to hold chukar; I look for them on the tops of ridges and in the "just about too nasty to walk in" type of terrain.

When hunting chukar, I pay particular attention to sounds. The familiar purr of the birds reminds me to keep my gun up; it also means that I'm busted so I'd better be ready to shoot.

The biggest problem with hunting on my lunch break is that I do not have my dog. Oh, man, does having a good pointer or flush dog make shooting chukar easier. I have had a chukar flush out from a bush I just stepped over; I literally could have stepped on it. Once, a good friend of mine was out gathering geodes in the cliffs of southern Idaho. When she was reliving herself near a bush, a covey of chukar busted out. After recovering from a heart attack, she noticed a dry spot in the center of the puddle and a set of bird footprints leading out of it. She had peed on one of the birds before they flushed.

That is the problem with the little beasties – they are unpredictable. They will either bust out at 80 yards or at 1 yard. It just depends on the day and how much they are hunted. In popular areas, like the WMA near my work, the birds tend to fly at long distances. For this reason I shoot bigger loads at them. My shot of choice for a chukar is a size 4 out of my 16 gauge. I get a lot of incidental hunting while on the chukar trail as well. I tend to get more cottontail rabbits and quail than chukar when chukar hunting.

When I manage to get a chukar on the ground, I take care to get to it immediately. I have found more than one wounded bird in a badger hole trying to escape.

The bird safe in my bag my thoughts turn to how I am going to enjoy it. My family loves a simple roasted bird dinner. But, roasting a game bird whole is always tricky: they tend to get tough in the legs and can dry out very easily. Of course, with the right combination of fat and moisture, it can be done.

I am a huge fan of the flavor of chukar. I find pheasant a little boring, like dry and tough chicken. Quail make me feel guilty for killing something with so little usable meat. But a chukar is like a Cornish game hen in the sky. They are the perfect size for one person to eat. Kill four and you feed four.

In this case, we are roasting a whole hen chukar. Pluck the bird...though to be clear, plucking a chukar is a pain in the butt, pure and simple. However, keeping the skin on a bird is critical for roasting. It keeps the moisture in and ensures a crunchy crust. The easiest way I have found to get the feathers off a chukar is to freeze the bird gutted, but whole. Don't pluck it yet, just gut the thing and toss it in the freezer. Then, after a few days of being frozen, take it out and let it thaw in the fridge. For some reason the feathers will pull right out. Trying to pluck a fresh chukar is an exercise in frustration – the skin rips. Even after freezing it you still need to be careful, as the skin is very soft, especially around the shot holes.

The best luck I have ever had plucking a chukar was when I tail-feather shot one and it ran head first into a rock. Because I had not damaged the birds' meat with the shotgun, I was able to pluck it.

Like a plucked duck, the chukar will have a few thin feathers that are best removed with a quick brush of a blowtorch. If you don't have a torch, a very quick pass under the broiler should singe off the remaining feathers. After the bird is torched make sure to wash it, otherwise it will taste of burnt feathers. Oh, and turn on the fan in the kitchen or open a window because the smell will be terrible.

When I prep a chukar for roasting, I cut the drumstick off above the knee joint to allow the meat to contract. This contraction makes the muscle on the leg thicker and less likely to dry out in the roasting process.

The next step is to stuff the bird with something with a lot of moisture, such as apples and onions. Early in the season a fresh peach half is perfect for one bird. The additional sugars from juicy fruit pair nicely with the game bird.

Cooked chukar requires additional fat. Roasting is a dry heat cooking method that can quickly rob meat of moisture. To compensate I will use high fat items, usually bacon. Another option is butter the bird under the skin.

Simple Roasted Chukar

A chukar is a white meat bird and needs cooked to 165°F. Cook until it reaches 155°F and then let rest for 5 minutes or so to finish cooking to the correct temperature.

Serves 1

1 plucked chukar
2 slices of bacon
½ small sweet apple
¼ small onion
½ teaspoon garlic powder
Salt and freshly ground pepper
1 tablespoon canola oil

Preheat oven to 425°F.

Season the skin of the chukar with salt and pepper. Heat canola oil in a medium-sized sauté pan and brown the bird on all sides. Remove from pan and let cool.

Slice onion and apple into half moon sections. Toss with garlic powder. Gently crush the onion and apple with your fingers and then stuff the mixture into the chest cavity of the bird. Be forceful when doing this, you can get more into the bird than you think.

Wrap the bird in the two slices of bacon, using one slice to help hold in the stuffing. Roast the chukar for 20-25 minutes. The bacon will be crispy and the juices coming off the bird should run clear.

10

SEASONING AFTER THE SEASON

I was lucky to be in this cold, snow-covered goose blind, or so I kept telling myself. My right boot had a hole in it and I was freezing my toes off. But I had accepted the late night phone call invitation – apparently the "normal" guy was out of town and the three-man blind had an opening. I had been on the short list for several years, but had never managed to get in, until now.

The morning started with setting out the decoys and fixing the blind. Our spread was good, about 100 decoys, all of them facing into the wind. We even had an empty section of the spread for the "kill zone." I was instructed not to "look up" at the geese as the captain called them in. I had always watched my game before, so this was weird; I had to simply trust that that goose could be shot when I was told. The suspense was unbelievable.

The last flock of geese was smart – they saw something about our decoy set up and didn't like it. Maybe they knew that we had the bodies of their dead brethren hidden under the hard plastic decoys. Maybe it was the slight skiff of snow that had formed; snow doesn't stick to the backs of real geese. Maybe it was all the human-sized footprints in the snow. They started to circle around, but would not commit to the landing. I was having a hard time not looking up at them – I could hear the wing flaps and honking – but I forced myself to look at my boots so as not to blow our cover.

One goose finally decided to come in for a landing, which caused a chain reaction. I heard "blast 'em" in my left ear. I jumped up and shot the goose farthest to the right, keeping my shooting "lane" in mind.

Two geese fell on that volley and it was 10 am, time to pack up. We'd shot a total of ten geese between the three of us – I was going home with three for myself. It was a good morning. I got back in time to watch cartoons with the boys and even cook a little breakfast.

Getting a good dose of protein in the morning is a great way to keep focused and healthy but when people think of breakfast, they rarely think of wild game. This is a shame considering most game meat packs more protein per ounce than the commonly consumed pig. One of my favorite breakfasts is a corned beef hash. Cured beef simmered in spices, salt and sugar and served with roasted potatoes – two eggs on top – nothin' is better.

Last year I was given a recipe for corning wild game. Remarkably it was very similar to my beef recipe. Well, duh. Anyway, I started with corning a venison roast and then moved onto smaller cuts. Eventually I landed on goose meat. It was a perfect fit.

For a lot of hunters, goose meat is a tough nut to crack – it often ends up in the smoker as jerky. I know why: it can be very gamey. I like the taste but understand how it can be a little over the top for some palates. An easy way to cure the gameyness from goose is to corn it – the brine cures the meat and changes the flavor and texture to that of the brine. Not a bad idea for those who don't want to waste the birds they shot.

Corned Goose

To corn a goose I use McCormick's pickling spice mix. While a purist might call this cheating I find it a heck of a lot easier to adjust a pre-done mix than keep fresh stocks of all the different seasonings that go into corned meat. To be honest, the package has a decent recipe for corned beef on it. To cure the goose meat I remove the breasts and reserve the leg meat. I cure only the breasts because they are easier to slice and there are no bones to remove.

A note about sodium nitrite – while you might not get botulism from curing meat this way on the off chance that you do it will be a horrible, excruciating and possibly lead to death. That said, I recommend the use of nitrites when making cured meat. It gives the meat a cool red color and without it the meat will be grey and kinda "blah" looking. Speed Cure or its equivalent can be found at most butcher shops.

Serves Many

2 quarts water
1 cup salt, I use kosher
½ cup sugar
1 oz. Speed Cure (Prague Powder or Insta Cure #1 work the same)
3 tablespoons pickling spices
6 goose breasts
1 large potato per pound of meat, ½ inch cubes
1 medium onion per pound of meat, diced
Fresh sage
Fresh thyme
Salt and freshly ground pepper
Red chili flakes

Bring the salt, sugar, Speed Cure and pickling spices to a boil. The boiling of the spices releases the oil and flavors that might not otherwise fully develop. Cool the brine to room temperature, (don't add meat to the hot liquid, it will start to cook and that can mess up the curing process). Not being one who likes to wait I have developed several methods of cooling the brine quickly after bringing it to a boil. One way is to cut the water amount that you bring to a boil in half and then add the remaining amount required in the form of ice at the end. For this recipe bring one quart of water to a boil and then at the end add one quart of ice (32 oz. of ice, measured by weight not by volume).

The method that I prefer is "ice wand cooling." I have a vacuum-sealed frozen gel pack that that I toss into brine. The ice pack drops the temperature very quickly; though make sure the vacuum seal is tight so you don't have funky blue liquid floatin' in the brine! When I am done cooling the brine I simply rinse off the gel pack and return it to the freezer.

Place the meat in the cooled brine, cover and move to the fridge. For a goose breast, about 1 pound each, brine for a minimum of 2 days (add 1 day curing per pound of meat).

Once the meat has cured rinse it off and let it air dry on a rack. Then add it to a vacuum bag with a little butter and seal it closed. Next place the vacuum-packed meat into a slow cooker on low for about 24 hours. The low temperature cooks the meat gently and the yield is typically higher than if the meat is simply boiled.

When the meat is cooked, it should be nice and tender. Cool it down in the bag; this will allow some of the juices to reabsorb into the meat. When cool, dice or slice the meat. Brown the onions in a cast iron skillet with a little oil. Then add the cubed potatoes. Simmer the mix for 15 minutes until the potatoes are cooked. Then add the corned meat. Toss in the fresh thyme and fresh sage and a pinch of red chili flakes for spice. Salt and pepper to taste.

11

THE BETWEEN SEASON

It happens about this time of year, every year: the "between season." The months drag on – you can't hunt ducks, grouse, deer, elk. Almost everything I hunt is closed. Except the lowly pigeon. It's always open season on pigeons in Idaho.

Most sportsmen think of the pigeon as a waste of good ammo and truthfully, for most of my hunting life, that is the way I regarded them as well. The pigeon has little value to most people. I have come to have a greater respect for hunting pigeons for three reasons. One, I get to see beautiful country when hunting them. Two, they are a challenge to hunt. And three, they provide good training for my dog.

Pigeons inhabit the most uninhabitable places you can imagine – in Idaho they make their homes in the cliff faces of our mountains. I hunt them in the Owyhee Mountain canyon lands. These rough cracks in the ground are perfect habitat for the birds. Sheer cliffs rise out of the desert floor and offer a protective habitat for the birds to roost and nest.

Beware when scouting pigeon areas, the steeper the better. For a good rule of thumb – if you can climb the rocks without a harness and pitons, go somewhere else. Pigeons like sheer, high cliffs. Most of the time I hunt pigeons from the bottom of the canyon. I find this easier than shooting them from the top of the rims. If I shoot from the rim of the canyon and I get a bird, I then have to go and retrieve it. If I shoot from the bottom, gravity does the work for me. The height of the cliffs often creates a problem while shooting. Birds can hover overhead but be over 200 feet away. Almost no shotgun is effective at that range.

A few things can be done to increase your odds for long shots on pigeons. First, use a tight choke on your shotgun – a full, extra full or super full are all good choices. When hunting the canyons for pigeons, I tend to keep a ridiculously tight choke in my shotgun. I use a Primo's "Tight Wad" choke that gets a 30-inch group at about 40 yards. That is tight enough to kill most turkeys so I figure that it should be good for pigeons.

I also recommend using a heavy load – size 4 shot. Unlike doves or barn pigeons, the canyon dwellers are going to be a ways away. Shooting a small load, like 8 shot, at a bird flying over your head at 60-70 yards is just a waste of ammo. So you need to be willing to shoot some heavier shot that will have enough kick to kill the birds at a long distance. It might seem like overkill to shoot at pigeons with pheasant loads, but they are bigger than you think and tougher than I like.

Shooting a box of shells at these birds in a day is not uncommon. They will multiply out of the cliff face when the shooting begins. Many times I have been tempted to shoot too far and too quickly at the birds. But one redeeming factor about pigeons is that they are not the smartest of creatures. They will, typically, circle back to their original location. So if you're willing to wait for another volley of shots, the pigeons will be back.

I also go pigeon shooting for my dog. When duck and goose season are over, I leave Miley at home during most of my hunting outings. It's not like I can wait in a ground blind with my ridgeback/lab mix and try and call in a turkey. But Miley, predictably, gets depressed, so I take her after the pigeons. She gets to work out her energy and I can get her field retrieving, flushing and locating birds. It's good practice for the fall upland game seasons. The dog needs to get in better shape and lord knows so do I.

So when the "between seasons" strikes go find a cliff and shoot some pigeons. Be ready and willing to hike into some beautiful but unforgiving territory for a bird most don't waste ammo on. Take the dog along for training. But mostly just remember that when your buddies complain about not being able to go hunting this time of year, you have a challenge waiting for them.

Baked Pigeon Enchiladas

This is a great recipe that helps hide the stronger flavors of an adult pigeon.

Serves 4

2 pigeons, skinned and deboned
7 oz. can salsa verde (plus one can of water)
½ 12 oz. can black beans, rinsed
10 oz. cheddar cheese, grated
5 flour tortillas
¼ red pepper, sliced
½ cup salsa
½ cup water or chicken stock
Salt and freshly ground pepper
1 teaspoon canola oil

Slice the pigeon meat into thin sections, cutting against the grain of meat. Heat the oil in a small soup pot over medium-high heat. Brown the meat and cook until well done. Add the can of salsa and an equivalent amount of water. Simmer on low for approximately 1 hour or until the bird is pull apart tender.

Preheat oven to 400°F. Remove pigeon from heat and cool slightly. Split meat mixture evenly between the tortillas and top with about 1 oz. of cheese and red peppers. Salt and pepper. Roll each tortilla and place, seam side down, in a 9 in. by 9 in. baking dish.

Mix ½ cup salsa and water together. Top the enchiladas with the remaining cheese and half the can of rinsed black beans. Then pour the salsa/water mixture over the casserole. Bake for 25-35 minutes.

LAND

The next morning my father and I crested the ridge
and stopped.
We glassed in the cool morning light;
the sun would be cracking over the mountains in a
few moments.
In the distance we saw the monster buck –
right where we thought he would be,
on the rim rocks.

12

ONE MORE STEP BACK

We spotted a monster buck the day before the season opened. He was a speck on the binoculars, but you could see that the speck had a hell of a rack.

Late season big buck hunting is a blessing and a curse. The blessing is that you get to go and get a big buck that you have been drooling over for the past few years. The curse is that the regular season hunters have already pressured every accessible square inch of the unit, hunting those damn 2x2's, by the time you get to hunt. The extra pressure makes the big bucks even smarter.

We stop and glass the buck for a while and I set the goal to harvest him. He is my old man of the desert, my white buffalo and my giant marlin all rolled into one. I need to get this buck to a secure location so that he will stay bedded down for the rest of the day – I'll have to trick him into going where I want him to go.

I choose some rim rock on the other side of the valley. Then I take a gamble. I figure that if I try to push him by walking straight at him and herding him toward the rim rock, I would lose him. He would do exactly what I did not want him to do, gallop off across open desert.

I moved positions about a mile back and came at the buck from the rim rock. The buck, instead of going out into the open desert, circled behind me and then disappeared into the rim rocks. I sat on a hill the whole rest of the day, waiting for him to leave. He never came out. I went back to camp hoping and praying that he would be somewhere near that location in the morning.

The next morning my father and I crested the ridge and stopped. We glassed in the cool morning light; the sun would be cracking over the mountains in a few moments. In the distance we saw the monster buck – right where we thought he would be, on the rim rocks. His head hung low but his walk was confident, ten does followed behind him.

We snuck within 150 yards and I pulled up and fired. I watched him drop down and then disappear behind a boulder. I knew the area and that he would have a rough time if he tried to travel far. We waited.

After about five minutes I walked toward the spot and found him lying on the ground, not 40 yards from where I had shot him. As I approached I set my rifle down and took off my gloves, his chest still heaving shallow breaths. The buck was a massive and regressing three pointer.

As I got closer, I noticed he started to shake a little and then climb to his front legs. I was about 5 yards away and I stopped in my tracks. The old man of the desert turned and faced me and like a Spanish bull he snorted and charged me.

I backpedaled as fast as I could, but the buck was gaining ground. One step: he was coming, dragging his hind legs behind him. Two steps: I was having a hell-of-a-time not tripping over the scattered sagebrush. Three steps: I stopped, braced like a football linebacker and caught his horns in my hands.

The buck was determined to gore me. I wrestled his thick-headed ass for a few seconds before realizing my stupidity. I needed an escape route, and fast. The buck was winning. I kicked my right boot out and tried to knock his front legs out from under him. I wish I could tell you that it worked.

Unfortunately, his front legs were like an old oak. And, I was now off balance. The buck pressed forward, using his horns as a weapon. As he thrashed he caught me with the tip of his right horn, tearing a hole in my shirt and in my stomach.

As I screamed, I saw my father out of the corner of my eye. He lifted his boot and kicked the animal square in the chest, knocking it over. I ran around behind the buck, ignoring my wound and the blood. With Dad's help, I sat on his back, held his head down to the ground, and slit his throat. The buck thrashed and knocked us off his broken back. He turned and looked at us, blood streaming from both sides of his neck. He tried to charge but couldn't; he stumbled and fell to the ground. The whole time he never looked away; he never gave in.

I stood, bleeding onto the desert rocks with the biggest buck of my life dead in front of me. It haunts me to this day. I feel horrible that I did not have a clean kill on the animal. On the other hand, I bet that this buck was proud to go out fighting. I will remember that hunt for the rest of my life. Not that I always want to, but I feel the scar in the shower every morning.

13

A BOY AND HIS BUNNY

The 20 gauge looks huge next to my oldest boy. The single shot is his now, a gift from Grandpa, and we are trying to get him his first rabbit. Or hare. Or whatever. The goal is for something that hops, has big ears and eats well.

Ok, so to be clear...the black-tailed jackrabbit is a hare, the cottontail bunny is a rabbit and the Snowshoe rabbit is also a hare – not at all confusing, especially to my 10 year old. The best way that I found to explain the difference is ear size. Big ears that make the bunny look funny, is a hare. Little ears, rabbit.

With that out of the way, my boy and I are out seeking the oft shot but seldom eaten black-tailed jackrabbit. These are big-ol-bunnies that weigh from 3-7 pounds. For years the moss backs would tell me that a jackrabbit is tough and inedible. I never questioned the wisdom of my elders until recently. I have started eating jacks in recent years and found that they are delicious. The meat on a jackrabbit is dark red and flavorful, not like the chickeny meat on a cottontail. And if I want chicken, I can buy chicken; I don't want my game meat to be bland. A big jack is tough as nails, but the little ones are very tender. I try to only shoot small jacks, but field judging a jackrabbit on the run is kind of hard.

My son and I walk noisily through the waist-tall sagebrush. We are deliberately trying to spook the jacks into running, or at least moving. It is not possible to sneak up on a jack – those ears are custom-tuned to locating predators. Unless you are a ninja the rabbit will probably hear you approaching before you see it. A running shot on them is not uncommon.

We spooked several from under our feet and saw several more running at about 100 yards. The nice part about jacks is that they typically only run short distances when they are not being actively pursued. I will whistle or clap to try and confuse the jack into stopping. When they stop running I tell the boy to shoot. I always try and keep a close eye on the rabbit when it stops. The coloration on jacks makes them virtually invisible under sagebrush. If they lose me in the brush I look for eyes, black dots, not for body outlines. Safety is the biggest concern, so the total number of shots so far has been limited. I don't let him shoot at moving targets just yet.

The best gun that I have ever hunted jacks with is an over-under .22/20 gauge. It had the range when needed and the scatter gun for up-close running shots. Currently I use either a side by side 16 gauge or an open sight single shot .22. The 16 is for when I want meat, the .22 is for when I want to go for a walk.

The boy finally lands a shot on a bunny stopped under a tall bush. The shot rolls the bunny, perforating its ears, hurting it enough for the boy to catch it in the bush with little effort and some lost skin. The glow in his eyes as he hoists his first rabbit, I mean hare, or whatever, is infectious. I think I just have created the local bunnies' worst nightmare.

How to Break Down a Rabbit

Skinning a rabbit is simple: the fur peels off like a banana peel. I make a small cut on the back of the bunny and then simply pull in both directions. The bunny is skinned.

Early in the season, the fur must be examined for little creatures. In the fall I tend to find warbles under the skin of cottontails. Warbles are larvae from a certain type of fly. They lay an egg under the skin and a maggot-looking creature grows. I have seen warbles the size of my index knuckle before. Yuck. Now, the warbles are not typically in the muscle of the bunnies but the meat does tend to be bruised under the infected site. I cut away the bruise before eating. Eating bunnies with warbles is safe.

Ticks are also commonly found on all types of bunny. They are typically off the rabbits shortly after the first hard freeze (usually October in southern Idaho). When I shoot a bunny in a tick month, I make sure to skin and gut them before I place them in my pack. I carry plastic grocery bags with me for this reason. I have found several ticks latched onto my upland game vest and even a few latched onto me when I forgot to remove the skin. It is also a good idea to use an anti-tick spray on the dog if using hounds to hunt the bunnies.

It's also a good idea to cook most rabbits/hares to well done, 150°F plus, because rabbits can pack a few nasty diseases around with them. The one that I fear most is the dog tapeworm, *Taenia pisiformis*, the concern is not for me but for my mutt. If the gut pile is eaten by the dog, it can get a nasty case of worms. Cooking them to well done ensures that almost all diseases on the animal are killed. According to the National Wildlife Health Center, rabbits and hares are edible year round. Yes, even in the summer.

When breaking down a hare, I get four separate cuts of meat. Two front legs, two hind legs, two loins and bones for stock. First, I de-articulate the back legs by "popping" out the ball joint on the hind legs then sliding my knife above the ball. The leg comes off clean with one cut. The front legs are easy as well; they are not even attached with bone. I simply slide my blade into the armpit of the bunny and make a quick cut.

To get the loins off I run my knife on either side of the backbone from the base of the neck to the tail. The blade should stop on the ribs of the hare. Then I press the meat away from the bone and slide the knife under the loin. It will come off in one large section. Think of it as a tiny little backstrap. The remaining bones and stomach flaps make great stocks and flavoring for soup.

For a rabbit I do the same process, except I do not remove the loins. I cut off the ribs at the backbone and then cut "saddle chops." A saddle is simply the loin still attached to the backbone.

I will fry all the separate pieces of a rabbit like chicken. The meat is white and tender. A hare is more complicated as the parts take different amounts of time to cook. I make soup or a slow roast out of the back legs. I will cube the loins and use as I would chicken. The front legs get saved until I have enough for a braised dish with sausage and potatoes.

Deboning the Hare Leg

The big back legs of a wild hare can be daunting. They are a working muscle and are NOT tender cuts of meat. So, what does a hunter do with them?

After removing the legs from the body, flip them so that the inside of the thigh is facing up. You will notice a line that follows the leg bone. Starting at the ball joint cut along this line until you reach the "knee" joint, then work the tip of the knife under the leg bone until it is free of the thigh.

When the bone is removed from inside the thigh, it will still be connected to the knee joint. At this point I use blunt force and twist the bone until I hear a crack of cartilage, then I will cut the connective ligaments and tendons and pull off the inside thigh bone.

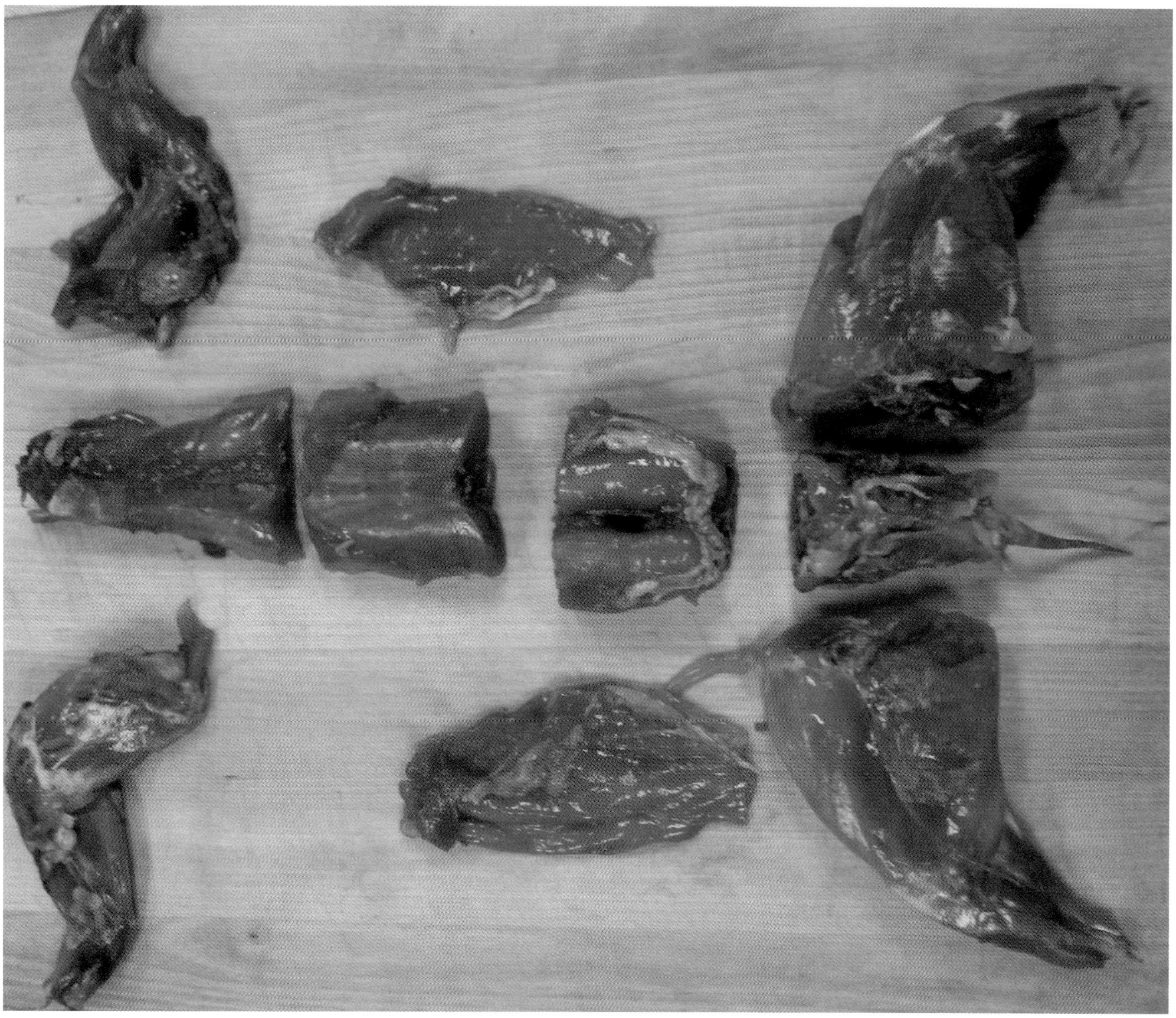

Chicken Fried Rabbit (or Hare, or whatever)

Serves 2

½ cup milk
½ cup buttermilk dressing
½ cup flour
½ cup corn starch
1 cup cracker crumbs, crushed fine
1 tablespoon Mrs. Dash Original Seasoning
1 tablespoon paprika
1 tablespoon cumin
Salt and freshly ground pepper
½ cup canola oil
1 lime, juice and zest

Pour the milk and dressing into a gallon-sized zip-seal bag. Mix thoroughly. Put the flour, corn starch, cracker crumbs, Ms. Dash, paprika, salt, pepper, and cumin in another zip-seal bag and toss to mix well.

Rinse the rabbit sections under the tap to wet and then move them to the cracker and seasoning mix. Press the sides of the bag to adhere the mixture to the meat. Dip the pieces in the milk.

Remove to a dry plate and then add back to the cracker crumb mix making sure to press some of the dry coating onto the flesh. When completely coated remove the rabbit sections and place on a clean plate, do not stack. This can be done up to 3 hours ahead of cooking.

In a medium sauté pan add oil to ¼ inch depth. Heat the pan for 5 minutes over medium-low heat. Add one section of the coated bunny, if the pan does not sizzle considerably then remove the section and turn the heat up a little. Brown the bunny sections, about 3-5 minutes, then flip. Most pans will have lost a considerable amount of heat by now so I make sure to turn the heat up to medium when I flip the sections. This allows for even browning.

Turn the heat down to low and pour off the remaining oil. Grab the largest section of rabbit and cut to the center to check doneness. Keep cooking if the meat is pink. The internal temperature needs to reach 150°F.

Right before serving sprinkle on the zest of the lime and then juice the lime over the top of the bunny. This will give the fried rabbit a little extra kick.

14

RABBIT SLAM

Each year when I see a turkey "Grand Slam" on TV, I pine for the experience. But I am a small game hunter to the bone, so I figured I could design my own slam, right? I hunt rabbits a lot so that seemed like a good starting place. This year I set out to get a Rabbit Grand Slam – I was going to hunt all four legal rabbit/hare species in Idaho – black-tailed jackrabbits, white-tailed jackrabbits, cottontail rabbits and snowshoe hares. To be clear, rabbits are not hares and hares are not rabbits, but all belong to the *Leporidae* family. Hare meat, including the black-tailed jackrabbit and the white-tailed jackrabbit, is darker and more flavorful than the chicken-y cottontail rabbit meat. Snowshoes are hares as well, but usually less red and closer to rabbit than hare.

Cottontails are predisposed to taste better – they do the least amount of running, eat green veggies, and are a white meat species. Snowshoes eat softer grasses and also tend to run small, making their meat all the more tender. For taste and texture, white-tailed and black-tailed jacks are a near tie; I think my family enjoys white-tailed jacks more because of the novelty. Both black and white tend to eat sagebrush and hard bark, not a culinary-friendly diet.

Each of these species has its own habitat so it makes the Grand Slam attempt all the more fun. Snowshoes are located in northern pine forests and often lurk in the darkest and thickest brush possible. I shot mine this year because it looked like snow had fallen inside a stump, but the cover was too thick for snow to reach that location. The hare stood out from the brown undercover; his pure white body was a beacon.

Black-tailed jackrabbits are sagebrush dwellers. With just a little cover, a little water and plenty of open spaces, jackrabbits thrive. I often hunt them on BLM private property boundaries near fields. They like the extra food and the fence lines provide a good shooting lane.

White-tailed jackrabbits are more elusive. They are often forced to high altitude ranges by the more aggressive black-tailed jackrabbits. I only see them in the headlights of my truck when I'm out mule deer hunting. These hares can get quite large and their white coat gets dirty in the winter. One December I was convinced that I had discovered an isolated population of snowshoe hares. I was wrong. They were just dingy white-tail jacks.

Cottontails are my nostalgia rabbit. I've hunted them since I can remember, mostly at the brahma bull ranch I grew up next to. We were not allowed to have guns on the ranch so we had to use wrist rockets and bows. The rabbits lived under farm equipment, in the blackberry patches, the trash pile and in the old ditch slag. It was quite a feat to come home with a rabbit that you killed with a rock and rubber band.

This fall I actively hunted rabbits, making special trips in search for each. I found it an inexpensive way to add a little game to my bird hunting, and some tension and uncertainty. For a bonus I would routinely run into quail, chukar, huns and grouse. It was terrible and SUCH a burden to have to hunt those while after my rabbits. This year I managed to get everything but a cottontail.

Rabbit with Mustard Sauce

First things first: you must brine a hare for this type of cooking. Unless you stick a jackrabbit in a slow cooker for 4-6 hours you are not going to get moist and tender meat. That said you can brine hare meat and fool everyone in 2 hours. Brining artificially overhydrates meat and makes it moist when cooked/overcooked.

Second thing – you must debone the hare leg. In the classic rabbit dish the thigh bone is left in., if this is done with a hare, it takes longer to cook.

Serves 2

The Brine

A brine is a salty water mix that adds flavor and moisture to meat. For hares, specifically the black-tailed jackrabbit, I brine for at least 24 hours.

1 quart hot water
⅓ cup salt
¼ cup brown sugar
1 clove garlic, smashed
1 sprig thyme
1 bay leaf
10 black peppercorns

Stir all ingredients into the hot water. Make sure the water is as hot as your faucet can produce, or even boil the water.

Let brine cool to room temperature. Add cut up rabbit to brine, making sure to cover all the meat with brine and place in the refrigerator. Let sit for 24 hours.

The Rabbit

1 rabbit (or hare) cut and brined, hare legs deboned
1 sprig thyme
1 tablespoon mustard
Salt and freshly ground pepper
½ cup all-purpose flour

Pat the brined rabbit dry with paper towels. Spread open the leg meat and place 1 sprig of thyme in each leg. Then spread half the mustard in each leg. Tie each leg closed. Season with salt and pepper. Roll the pieces in flour and reserve on a dry plate.

Heat half the butter or oil in a medium sauté pan with a lid. When fat is hot, but not yet brown, add 2 or 3 of the rabbit pieces. Cook on each side 2-3 minutes until a golden crust has formed. Remove from pan and keep warm. Repeat with remaining meat.

Mustard Sauce

2 tablespoons butter or olive oil
½ small red onion, finely diced
1 cup white wine (something good, drink the remainder during dinner)
Water
½ cup heavy whipping cream
3 tablespoons Dijon mustard
4 sprigs thyme

Add onion to the pan. Let cook for 3 minutes then put the meat sections back into the pan. Pour in the white wine. Lower heat to a simmer and cover pan with a tight-fitting lid. Simmer for one hour checking the moisture level every 10 minutes or so, adding more water if needed. Check meat to see if it is tender. If the rabbit or hare is more than a year old, it will probably take more time.

Continue to add water and check tenderness until the meat is sufficiently tender. It is done when the meat is falling off the bone. This should take no more than 2 hours.

Remove meat from pan, keep warm. Increase heat to medium high and boil the remaining liquid. Add the cream, mustard and thyme. Reduce heat to a simmer and reduce the mixture to a sauce consistency. This should only take 3-4 minutes. Taste the sauce, salt and pepper as needed. When the sauce tastes good add the rabbit legs back to the pan, turn off the heat and cover. Let sit for 3 minutes. Move legs to a platter and pour sauce over the top, garnish with fresh thyme.

15

TO MY SHOULDER IN ELK

I have blood on my hands, under my fingernails. Hell, it is all the way up to my shoulder. I am trying with all of my might to pull the soccer-ball sized heart from a dead cow elk. I spooked her from her high desert country bed. She was dead only minutes when I found her, so I said a thank you prayer and began the awful but necessary process of evisceration.

A sickening sound, like wet Tupperware losing its seal, signifies the heart is free. I breathe a sigh of relief and stash in a zip-seal bag (I carry several of them for just this purpose). The animal will now start to cool and is a lot less likely to spoil. I work off quarters of the animal: cutting at the ball joint and disarticulating each hind quarter off, leaving the skin on to maintain a protective barrier from the dirt and pine needles all around. I am making progress but I'm still in trouble.

Let me back up a little.

This elk was a total surprise. I had been hunting the opposite hillside and glassed the hill for hours. I was convinced that it was barren, so when something came crashing through the brush I jumped out of my skin.

The long hike inspired me to daydream of other things, mostly cold beer I'm afraid. I watched as a cottontail rabbit bounced across the shale in front of me. I shouldered my .270 and grabbed a rock to toss at Mr. Rabbit when the elk crashed out of the brush.

It took me a minute to get my bearings and remember that I was elk hunting. Luckily for me elk have a habit, to their potential detriment, of running a perceived safe distance and then turning back to look at their pursuer. For a hunter this is a great shot opportunity. And, as expected, the cow stopped at 80 yards and turned to look at me.

I saw she was with another cow, a yearling and a small raghorn bull. Four elk.

She was clearly the lead cow of the group, probably the mother of both the bull and the yearling. She stood in front of her family and gave me the skunk eye. I gave her a .270 shell in the side. Or so I thought. But she just stood there – no stumble, no wince of pain – had I missed her completely? I found this hard to fathom as I was using a shooting stick and she was less than 100 yards away.

It has always been my personal philosophy to "shoot until the damn thing falls over." So, as she turned to run, I pulled up again, and fired. Like ghosts, the elk disappeared into the brush. True to their nature the small herd stopped to look at me again, this time from about 250 yards in a small clearing on the opposing hillside. Two yearlings, a cow and bull. Four elk.

I had my sights on the lead cow again but my gut was telling me something was wrong. If I had missed the cow at 80 yards, what right did I have in shooting at her again at 250? Why were there now two yearlings when before there was only one? If I had hit her, and I was almost positive that I had, then I would find blood and an elk. With an elk in my sights and finger on the trigger, I pulled my gun off my shoulder. I hoped like hell I had not wasted the only chance I would get all season to tag out. What if that was my elk and she was now cresting, injured, over the side of another hill? God knows the last thing I needed was to shoot two elk.

I walked toward the direction of my shot, hoping for blood. In ten short steps I saw what looked like a dead horse under a tree. My gut dropped out of my belly. Luckily I had held my shot.

When I reached the dead elk I said a short prayer, thanking her for the sustenance that she would provide my family. I know that the prayer means nothing to the dead elk, but it means something to me and praying after death is a cathartic response. The praying was for me, as much as for the elk. I had just committed murder and now had a ton of work to do.

After roping the cow's hind legs to nearby trees to gut her, I found that both of my shots had landed in her "wheelhouse" – the platter-sized vitals section behind the front shoulder. My shooting had been fine. This was simply one tough lady elk.

And this big ol' gal was the reason I was in trouble.

I was miles away from any road and I was supposed to be meeting the rest of my hunting party shortly. My "little walk" out of a finger draw had unexpectedly turned into a successful hunt. I had meat down and not just a little bit. Cow elk, on average, weigh about 500 pounds.

After storing the organs I placed one back quarter in my hunting pack, and tossed it onto my back. The weight was crushing: 60-70 pounds of elk and 20 pounds of gear and water. I peed a circle around my kill to ward off the coyotes and began my ascent out of the hole, hoping to catch the rest of my party. Otherwise, it was going to be a long, long night of hauling meat.

One foot in front of the other was my mantra, but at points I thought that my legs would actually catch fire. I had been training for hunting season all summer so I was in good physical condition, but I was still a hurting unit.

Like most hunting excursions, I have to work for my reward. And my reward was the massive amount of food in my pack and more on the ground waiting to be retrieved. The chef in me wanted to build a fire and roast a hunk of meat right on the spot. The pragmatist in me knew I needed to get back to the camp and recruit some help.

My fellow hunters were running late so I left a note, grabbed my pack frame and headed back to the kill. Soon enough I heard a shot being fired from the direction of camp. I shot into the air, and another shot rang out in the distance. Primitive echolocation, but it worked. Eventually I heard voices, and I called out – when they returned the call I knew that life had just gotten easier.

Several trips later and the elk was in the back of my SUV and I was headed home. I had donated one of the tenderloins to the camp party but I could not stay the night – I was expected at work in a few short hours.

I don't know that I have ever felt so good about being so tired at work. It was totally worth it.

Elk Shank with Red Wine and Rosemary

If I could shoot one animal per year to stock my freezer it would be a nice, youngish, cow elk. They are perfect table fare: tender, flavorful and ample in proportion, they are like giant whitetail deer. Of course, with a large animal there is always scrap and trim to be used and it's not always obvious to know the best way to utilize those parts. For instance: shank meat. Shank meat is ungodly tough, right? Yes, it's a tough piece of meat but it is easy to make shine. Think of all those fancy restaurants serving lamb shanks like hotcakes and charging upwards of $35 a plate. Connective tissue, the same thing that makes the shank tough, is what makes it delicious. That tissue, if cooked long enough, melts into a buttery, luscious sauce. The naturally occurring gelatin breaks down and incorporates into the cooking liquid. But only if you give it time. Shanks are slow food. Mmmm, tasty slow food. Anyway, enough science, how about a recipe?

Serves 4

1 elk hind shank, deboned, bone reserved
½ cup all-purpose flour
2 tablespoons butter
Salt and freshly ground pepper
1 white onion, chopped
2 large carrots, peeled and chopped
10 cloves garlic
10 sprigs fresh rosemary
2 cups red wine
2 tablespoons fresh thyme

Preheat oven to 300°F or turn on a slow cooker to "low" setting.

Roll the deboned shank meat in the flour. Heat butter in a large cast iron Dutch oven over medium heat. Brown the shank meat on all sides. When browned add the onions and any remaining flour to the pan. Season with salt and pepper. Stir onions around to avoid flour clumps from forming.

Add the carrots, garlic and half of the rosemary. Let cook for 1 minute and then add the red wine to "deglaze" the pan (deglaze means to remove the brown bits from the bottom of the pan – those are good things). When at a boil add enough water to just cover the meat, approximately 2 quarts depending on the size of the pan. Cover tightly and move to the oven. Cook 4-6 hours or until the shank is fork tender. Remove from the oven.

You will now be faced with a dilemma – serve the shank hot or cool and serve the next day. Braised meat, as a rule, is always better the next day – it's had time to settle and absorb flavors. Either way, whenever you decide to eat the shank remove the meat and reduce the sauce over medium-high heat. Add the remaining rosemary and the thyme as it thickens. This will brighten up the whole dish. Serve over Hattie's Mashers or polenta for a great, rib-sticking meal.

16

LIVER AND ONIONS

When I was about 8-years-old, I stayed with my aunt and uncle for a few weeks during the summer. They lived by the tracks, had chickens and a whole lot of broken-down cars in the back lot. My uncle was an old-time farm boy and loved his "liver n' onions" once a week.

He was also kind of a hard ass, as in the kind of guy that makes his 8-year-old nephew eat overcooked liver with black onions and packaged gravy once a week. If I didn't eat it all at dinner he would microwave it for me for breakfast and make me choke it down before my pancakes. It took me 15 years to try a slice of liver again after that summer. Only when I had a properly cooked deer liver did I ever come to appreciate its culinary value.

I was still in college when I shot a little buck that would become my first slice of liver in a long time. I watched him crest the mountain top and then drop below the ridgeline. I snuck up on him and took my shot. Not a clean kill, but a kill. When my father and I got to the buck, he glanced over his shoulder toward the truck, and said, "Good luck. See you at bottom with the four-wheeler."

So there I was, my first deer in quite a few years, alone with a knife. No more instructions from Dad. No help getting the deer off the hill. "Okay, I get it, time to man up and do this right." I eviscerated the buck on a small incline. Knowing that my family always liked the heart I wrapped it in a grocery sack and stuffed it in my pack. Then, looking at the gut pile, I dug out the liver. I can't tell you why but I just felt like I should; like I should use the buck in every way that I could.

I taped an orange hat to the horns and a tarp to the butt and tossed the buck over my shoulders. I walked out, carrying the deer in one load, blood soaking the back of my jacket and my collar-length hair. I could see the look of surprise in my father's eyes when I came through the brush. He saw his boy, and he saw a man. A man that was going to, apparently, eat some liver.

When I slapped the liver down on the cutting board of the restaurant I was working at, the chef looked at me like I was crazy. It was a fish house. He came over to inspect my work, nodded in approval and said, "Whatever you do, don't cut that into little strips, it'll ruin it."

I was puzzled. Thin, overcooked slices of liver were all that I had eaten. And what I was preparing myself to choke down. The chef instructed me to cut the liver into thick steaks.

"Cook it like a steak, medium rare, and the liver will be smooth. Onions will make sense in the dish."

I did as he said, and Chef was right. From then on liver has been a staple in my diet.

Inspection is the first step in insuring a good liver meal. If it is spotted or has other odd looking things on or in it, give it a toss. Different types of bugs (flukes) can infest the livers of big game animals and I have no intention of swallowing those creatures. Also, the livers of old animals can hold toxins, according to some, and should be avoided. I also find that the livers of older animals tend to have more of the "mineral" flavors some find offensive. The liver from young bucks doe's make the best eating, but we all knew that.

When dressing a big game animal, I always try and save the heart and the liver for prompt eating. Both should be placed in gallon-sized zip-seal bags and put on ice or cooled as soon as possible.

I like to let a heart soak in a bowl of salt water in the fridge for a good 24 hours before cooking. Hearts, when overcooked, can be incredibly tough. Giving the muscle a little brine will help impart flavor and also keep it from cooking as fast.

With hearts, I also make sure to rinse the valves out as much as I can. I will manually "pump" the heart with my hand while running it under the faucet to get as much of the coagulated blood out as I can. If the heart is not to be consumed within a day or two, it should be vacuum-sealed and frozen.

Liver is best the day after harvest or it should be frozen. Usually I cut the liver into smaller sections that allow me, and only me, to have a liver meal. I don't force liver down my children's necks, like my uncle did to me, so my solo enjoyment gets stretched out.

Liver and onions is a classic, down-home, blue-plate, country club bridge player honky café meal. Often disrespected in preparation by being sliced thin and overcooked into a hunk of chalk. Loved by some, reviled by others. Here is how to make a convert to the liver and onion cause.

Pan Roasted Liver with Sweet Onions

Serves 2

Roux

Roux is the classic thickening agent for most western dishes. Keeping a little on hand is not a bad idea.

½ cup butter
½ cup all-purpose flour

Melt the butter in a small sauce pan over medium heat. Turn heat to low and add the flour in small batches. Cook the mixture for 2-3 more minutes -it should be a thick paste at this point. The roux is best used cold so reserve it in a small container in the refrigerator.

Semi-Demi-Glace

1 12 oz. can low-sodium beef stock
¼ cup good red wine
1 sprig fresh rosemary
2 tablespoons roux

Combine the beef stock, wine and rosemary in a small saucepan, bring to a simmer. Cook until reduced by half. Stir in the cold roux, a little at a time, until the mixture thickens. Reserve.

The Liver

2 4 oz. liver portions
1 red onion, thinly sliced
¼ cup Balsamic vinegar
1 tablespoon butter
Salt and freshly ground pepper
1 tablespoon of canola oil

Melt the butter in a small saucepan and add the onions. Cook on low until the onions are translucent, about 15 minutes. Add the vinegar and cook until the onions are completely black and all liquid is absorbed, about 10 minutes. Keep warm.

Pat liver dry. In a medium sauté pan add the oil and heat, on medium high, until the oil is almost smoking. Add the liver. Brown for 3 minutes (or longer). Flip and brown reverse side. Check the internal temperature. When the liver reaches 120°F remove from the pan and place on a paper towel to rest. DO NOT cook above 130°F.

Place ⅛ cup of the semi-demi-glace in a small circle. Add half of the onions. Slice the liver and fan on top of the onions. Serve with a nice red and grilled vegetables.

17

MAKING PRAIRIE GRIZZLIES TASTE GOOD

It took me a while to understand the dialect of the shop workers when I first heard them talking about Indian Crick in the back of the plant. I never questioned the pronunciation of the woodcutters; it was not my place. But I did question my father.

He explained to me the crick vs. creek distinction, "A creek is something that you are proud of," he said. "A crick is, well, something that you're not proud of...and that is definitely a crick behind the plant."

Indian Crick in Nampa is full of old cars, mattress springs and retired refrigerators, not to mention broken up slag from concrete ditches.

In addition to being the town dump, Indian Crick is known for housing a large population of rock chucks – the soft streamside dirt and the ample cover afforded by the trash make it a perfect setting for the dirty little buggers. Maybe too perfect. Infestation has become a problem at the plant and so, every year an employee is asked to "correct the population" as best as they can. Shooting a high-powered rifle at the little beasties is not an option, according to HR. So each year a bowhunter at the plant gets to come on the property over the weekend and take care of the pests.

This year my father was the person selected to alleviate the problem and by nothing more than simple association, so was I.

In springtime, the rock chucks emerge from a long hibernation and explore the world around them to stave off the hunger pains. The best time to hunt them is during that critical emergence point. They are complacent due to hunger and less concerned about humans.

The second best time to strike is when the babies come out. They present a smaller target, but are significantly dumber than their larger relatives. One trick to harvesting a larger number of babies it to scare the adults into their holes by tossing rocks at them. The adults pop their heads up to chirp warnings at the pups and all of a sudden it's "Whack-a-Mole" time. When one pups goes into a hole, another one pops up.

Sounds brutal, but when the chucks are tearing apart the foundation of 200 people's livelihood certain liberties should be taken.

Shooting the chucks with traditional bows offered up a few challenges, not least of which was the loss of arrows: the concrete slag was far more prevalent than our plump little targets. I was breaking arrows with every other shot. I split several cedar shafts hoping for a *Marmota flaviventris* to meet its demise.

Unlike a rabbit, the beasts wouldn't nonchalantly die, a few paces after being hit – the judo points just seemed to bounce off the hides of the large rodents. "Using a judo point on a rock chuck is like trying to gut a deer with a butter knife," my dad remarked, "While it might work eventually there's got to be a better way." Stupidly, we were using deer hunting arrows for a varmint. I figured it cost me about $10 per shot when I broke an arrow. After about three arrows I had had enough!

After that we switched to broadhead points. Dad and I scrounged up every old broadhead we could find and scoured our shafts to find those a little too short or improperly tuned. Then we lobbed arrows into rock piles with abandon.

I remember one large chuck that was making his home in a combination bed frame/car hood. He would climb to the edge of the frame that hung out over the water to peer out at the world. I snuck in close, drew and let my improved equipment fly. The arrow made a "ping" noise as it struck the bed frame; toothpick-sized hunks of cedar flew into the air around the chuck. The chuck got away.

The chucks seemed to have no less of a fighting spirit, even with the deadlier equipment. They even seemed spiteful toward us. When they would come out across the crick we would make a calculated judgment and fling an arrow. If we missed and the shaft did not break on impact in the concrete, it would bury itself in the dirt, which also happened to provide the perfect soil conditions for stinging nettle. I would don my duck hunting waders, gloves and a long sleeve shirt to go arrow fetching.

One day, we didn't have necessary equipment to fetch the arrows so we figured we would just come back in the morning. Upon our return we found the shaft of our arrows chewed in half – a case of rock chuck revenge! Every shaft left unattended was eaten. They chewed on nocks, chewed off hand-glued turkey feathers and ate custom cedar shafts.

One particularly nasty chuck had the audacity to chew on my arrow while skewered and floating down the crick – we found him later with the arrow still sticking out his side and growling at us from a tree branch. Talk about tough.

Then we had to figure out what to do with the dead ones. If we just chucked them in the crick we were no better than the other litterbugs. We couldn't just toss them in the dumpster either.

One of my brilliant ideas for body disposal was to eat the rock chucks. I had no illusions that I was going to make a culinary masterpiece out of the large rodents, but I am a chef…so, why the hell not try?

After a few had been dispatched and the bodies recovered, I set to the task of gutting and skinning them.

Honestly I have field-dressed a mule deer in less time than it took to clean those chucks. The skin is tough as iron and even with frequent knife sharpening I was never able to make quick progress. Just puncturing the skin was almost impossible, then, unlike most other creatures I have skinned, the hide would not release from the muscle. Rock chucks deserve the nickname "prairie grizzly" and all the connotations that go with it. I am just glad they are not any bigger.

Anatomically chucks are different than other game animals. The rodents, being a burrowing species, are very front heavy as opposed to the hindquarters being the main protein source. The little buggars have virtually no backstrap or loin and most of the weight was in internal organs and fat. They look like fat and lazy buggars and looks are not deceiving. In addition, the fat on the outside does not translate to fat on the inside of the muscle. These were not going to be tender meat.

Knowing that the animal is going to be tough determines my cooking method. In this case I decided "slow and low" would work best. I cooked the rock chuck in bacon fat and canola oil.

The meat was soft and not gamey – kind of like dark, garlicky pulled pork. Good enough that I was inspired to add rock chuck to the dinner menu at home. I thought tricking my family might be the best first step in convincing them to eat the rodents, so, I made a rock chuck pizza. Seriously, what kid does not like a pizza? Smiles at the table turned to grimaces as soon as I told the family what they had eaten. One night on the couch was worth all the looks at the dinner table. I was forgiven by morning.

Rock Chuck Confit

To confit something means to cook it in fat for a long time, very slowly. When you cook something very slowly in fat the connective tissue, the stuff that makes the animal tough, breaks down. To confit something you need to follow three basic steps: cure the meat in salt, brown the meat, then poach it in oil. To confit meat is both a cooking and preservation method: salt creates a hostile environment for micro-organisms and then cooking the meat in hot oil kills any microbes that are still alive. Top that off with a layer of microbe-inhibiting fat covering the meat and you can keep confit for up to 6 months in your fridge.

Prior to curing the rock chuck meat clean it very well. Then pat the meat dry with a paper towel and remove any remaining fur or blood.

Dry Rub (quantities are per pound of meat)

⅛ cup salt
1 tablespoon freshly ground pepper
1 tablespoon garlic powder

Mix salt, pepper and garlic powder in a small bowl. Rub the meat with the mixture, place in a cake pan or bowl and cover with a towel. After 24 hours rinse the meat off and pat it dry with a paper towel.

2 tablespoons canola oil

In a large sauté pan heat 2 tablespoons of canola oil over medium-high heat. Brown the meat on all sides. Remove from pan and place in casserole dish or cake pan.

Confit

1 cup rendered bacon fat (optional)
Canola oil
8 cloves of garlic
16 black peppercorns
2 bay leaves
2 sprigs fresh rosemary
4 sprigs of fresh thyme
10 fresh sage leaves

Preheat oven to 350°F.

Place the garlic, pepper, bay leaves, rosemary, thyme and sage on top of the browned meat. Add the bacon fat and pour just enough canola oil to cover the meat. Tightly wrap the pan in aluminum foil and place it on a cookie sheet.

Bake for 1 hour and then set the oven temperature to "warm." Cook on warm for 3 hours. Turn off the oven and let the meat cool inside the oven for one hour.

Transfer the meat into quart jars making sure it is completely submerged in fat. Cool the jars uncovered in the refrigerator until completely cool. Cover and refrigerate for up to 6 months.

Rock Stickers

Serves 4

Filling

½ pound rock chuck confit, shredded
1 tablespoon minced garlic
¼ cup green onions, sliced
½ small red onion, minced
¼ cup fresh cilantro, minced
¼ cup Napa cabbage, thinly sliced
10 fresh mint leaves, thinly sliced
1 teaspoon Sriracha
1 tablespoon oyster sauce
1 dash soy sauce
1 tablespoon sweet chili sauce
1 egg, well beaten
Salt and freshly ground pepper, to taste

Mix all ingredients in a small bowl until fully incorporated.

½ cup water
2 tablespoons corn starch
20 pot sticker wrappers
¼ cup canola oil

Make a slurry out of the water and corn starch. Place 3 tablespoons of the filling in the center of a wrapper, brush the edges with the corn starch slurry. Fold one corner of the wrapper to the center of the filling. Move to the next corner of the wrapper and fold that to the center as well. Repeat until you have a stop-sign-shaped packet. Flip the pot sticker over so that the slurry wets the wrapper and creates a seal.

Heat ¼ cup of oil in a large non-stick pan. Add the pot stickers one at a time, seal-side down first. Fry in the pan until golden brown then flip and brown on the other side.

18

ANTI-LOAP

I had spent the better part of an hour belly crawling onto four antelope. At first I thought the alkaline soil near Gooding seemed devoid of life; I assure you the ground is covered in thorns and little else. As I write this I am still able to pick them out of my palms. I caught sight of the antelope from the road. I stopped to glass a promising section of ground. After I glassed the "good area", I turned around and caught the antelope bedded on the sagebrush boundary near a canal.

To sneak onto the bedded pronghorns, I would need to belly crawl roughly 400 yards before I felt comfortable shooting. Game time.

I approached the area I had designated a reasonable shooting distance and I brought myself up from my belly, slowly to my knees and then to a sitting position. I scoured the brush where the antelope had been laying. Had they been bumped, to where? Then, out of the corner of my eye, I caught movement at a half mile off, four antelope cresting a ridgeline and never looking back.

This was the fifth time that day I had been busted by speed goats. I was getting sick of not being able to get within 400 yards. Earlier I had learned that I could not shoot at that range…I watched a cloud of dust puff at the feet of a doe. I had shot at her with my .270, a good flat shooting rifle and the bullet fell a full 3 feet. She was too far, I knew it, but I shot out of frustration anyway. Not my best moment.

I pivoted on my butt and looked back in the direction of my truck, thinking to take a water and snack break. That is when I saw something that pissed me off. A herd of antelope were walking down the same road I'd driven in on. I counted forty-two goats at one point, marching single file past my Ford. My chocolate lab, Reed, was in the back. (This was a November hunt, don't worry it was not hot for the dog. Plus he is lazy; he almost likes the truck more than hunting. Unless it's for ducks.) I heard Reed bark at the antelope as they passed; they were indifferent to him.

They kept moving slowly, even though they knew I was present. I would shuffle and one or two antelope would stop and look at me. I was busted, sitting in the open. All I could do was count them as they passed and laugh at the irony of it all.

When they had crested over the next small ridge, I stood up and ran back to my truck. All I could hope for was to crest in time for a shot on the herd. Yeah, no, that didn't happen. As soon as I appeared over the ridge, the antelope disappeared into the distance.

That made six times being busted.

But then my phone came to the rescue. It was about 3 pm and I was spent. I'd logged about 8 miles on my legs looking for speed goats. As I drove out I caught sight of a large herd of antelope feeding below some rim rock at about a mile off. I stopped the car and glassed them. There was absolutely no way to approach them from the front without being seen. If I tried, all I would get was a seventh busted moment.

Not being familiar with the ground, I pulled the Map App up on my phone. The little blue dot dropped on my location and I could see the rim rock the antelope were holding on. I zoomed out and saw a four-wheeler trail that circled above and behind the antelope.

I dropped a pin on the location and set off in search of the two-track. I found it and drove it to its end. I was still a solid mile from the antelope's location, but I was willing to walk that. I slowly made my approach, the wind blowing up-hill and into my face.

The little blue dot was getting closer and closer as I walked to my goal. I never, not even once, thought that the antelope would still be within range. Precedent was against me. Then I saw one, then another, and then the whole herd appeared below the rim rock. They were about 150 yards out.

Having a doe-only tag I pulled up on a nice looking female and set my sights. Then I noticed two smaller antelope following behind her. I could not kill this doe; she still had fawns that needed her enough to follow her around. As my buddy so eloquently put it after the hunt, "You wanted to have steak and sleep too, I get that." Quickly I had another doe in my scope. This one at 100 yards.

One shot and she fell. Clean kill and instant antelope heaven.

I had to scramble down the rock face to get to my kill. Frustratingly, the antelope that I could not get closer than 400 yards to earlier that day hung around at about 75. I could have picked one, any one, from the herd. Instead it was time to eviscerate the animal.

When I looked closer at my doe, it was apparent that she had recently been in a fight with a barbed-wire fence. Her hide was scraped and large sections of her neck were hairless, luckily no active infections were detectable.

Hauling her onto my shoulders, after she was gutted, I struggled the mile back to the truck. The sun was setting and I had my first antelope tag punched. It was the end to a perfect day of hunting. When I got home I knew more work was to come; I had to butcher this animal.

Antelope Meat Care

"Cool those darn things off," is the consensus among pronghorn hunters. Antelope run at a high temperature, about 105°F, higher than most other big game species, making it critical to gut them fast under the hot sun of archery season – skin them as soon as possible and to have them on ice in two hours or less or the meat will foul. It is improper treatment, I believe, that gives speed goats their bad reputation for being a gamey meat.

Cool quickly and then age the animal for a few days. Tenderness in any meat is determined by three things 1) the age of the animal 2) the amount of use and 3) fat content. The age of an animal will invariably determine the tenderness of the meat – an old rut buck's meat will be a heck of a lot less tender than that young doe in the freezer. Wild game animals that roam large areas tend to have less tender meat. A buck that spends his whole life in the same 120-acre cornfield will be a lot more tender than one that migrates through a hundred miles of pine trees each year. Lastly, wild game is naturally low in fat.

To combat an inherent lack of tenderness, I recommend aging big game meat. Aging counteracts the "age" of the animal and the "amount of use" issues mentioned before, at least to some extent. Then fat can be added in the cooking process.

Aging meat breaks down the tough connective tissue in the animals' muscles. The connective tissue is made up of strands of collagen. Naturally occurring enzymes will start to break down the collagen over time. Most butchers agree that hanging a deer for 5-7 days, in a 40°F cooler, is plenty of time for the meat to get tender.

The easiest way to screw up meat it to age it at the wrong temperature – your 60°F garage is no place "hang" meat for more than a day or two. Bad bacteria grow exponentially at temperatures above 45°F. Properly aging meat starts with cooling the meat on ice in the game bags used in the field. Once home, rinse all the meat off and wash the game bags, then put the meat back in the clean bags and ice again. Rotate the meat every day, draining any water build up. Age your pronghorn about 4-5 days, any longer and you risk rot.

Properly aging wild game meat will lead to a much more pleasant eating experience. Just remember to keep it clean, keep it cold and keep it rotating.

Butchering an Antelope Leg

Butchering one's own meat has gone from the economical option on the farm to hip and trendy. Butchers are the new celebrity chefs. Hell, I have taught classes on meat fabrication to men in skinny jeans and well-groomed beards. Apparently, DIY butchering is a thing now.

As hunters and anglers, we owe it to ourselves to butcher what we kill. We need to own this skill in the true sense of "I was doing it before it was cool" mentality. Sure, butchering takes time. Sure, it is kind of a pain in the ass. But taking that next step and placing meat that you hunted, butchered and cooked on the plate is immensely satisfying. And, if done right, much better tasting.

With most wild game, big game in particular, the hindquarters are the major meat source. Knowing how to breakdown a hindquarter of game is an essential butchering skill.

The first step in butchering an animal is to make sure it is clean. I wash the legs in my kitchen sink under cold water. I pick off stray hair, little chunks of forest floor and leaves. Then I pat the leg dry with a clean kitchen towel.

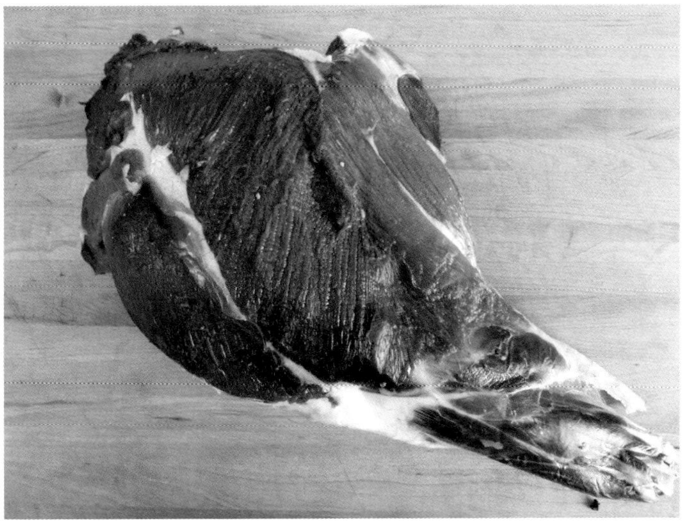

Place the hindquarter ball-joint down on the cutting board.

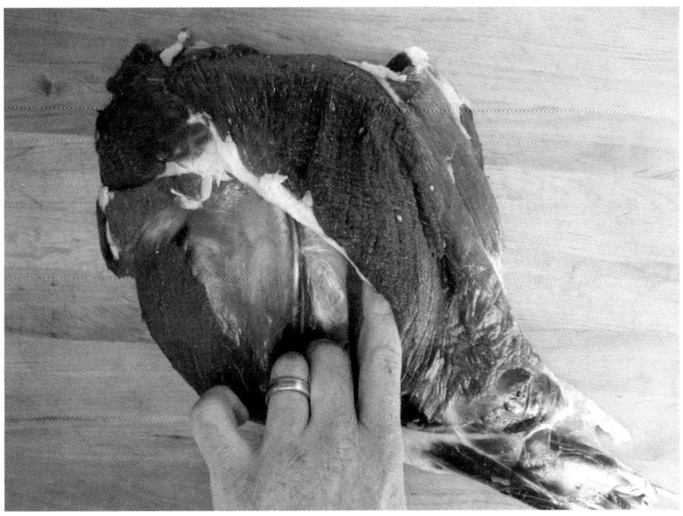

Find the large seam running down the outside of the leg. This is the top round and it is draped over the sirloin tip. Take two fingers and increase the size of the seam.

Use the tip of a knife to separate the top round off the hind leg.

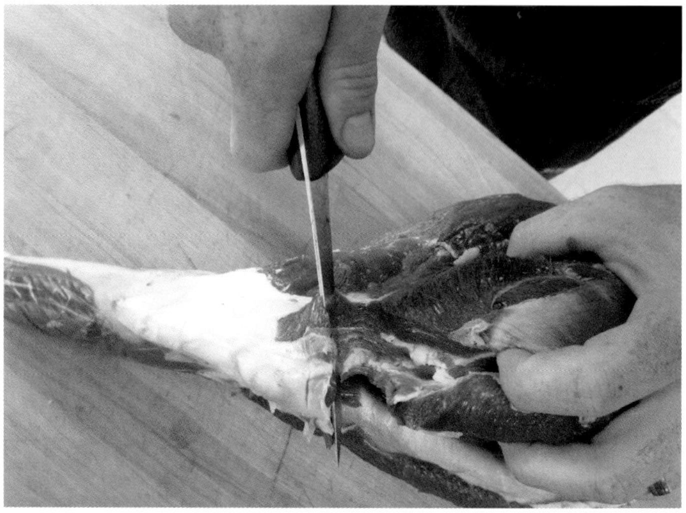

When the top round (eye of round is still attached) is removed, take your knife and cut along the top of the shank joint, just above the major amounts of sinew. Circumnavigate the joint with the knife; the lower section will be the shank cut.

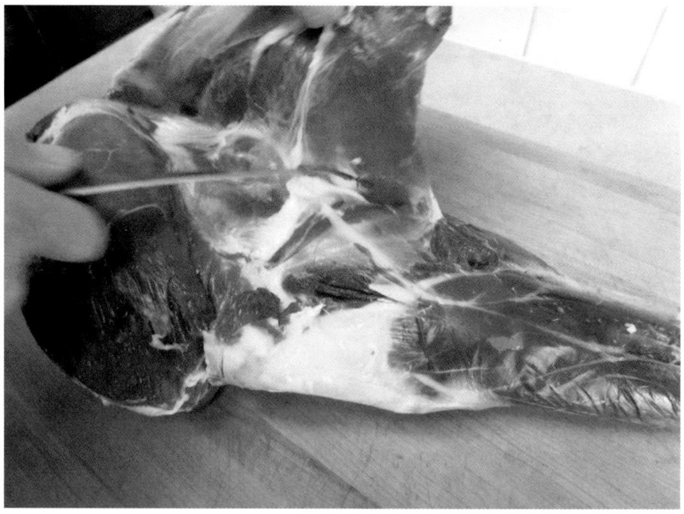

Follow the sirloin tip down to the bone, slice along the bone. Don't go too fast, lots of meat is often left on the bone unnecessarily.

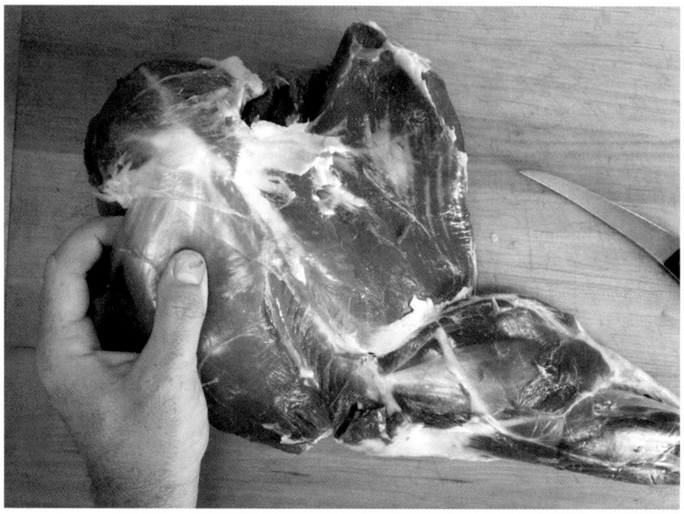

Carefully work the bone clean of the meat on both the Sirloin Tip side and the bottom round side. If you do this, the bone should come free of the meat.

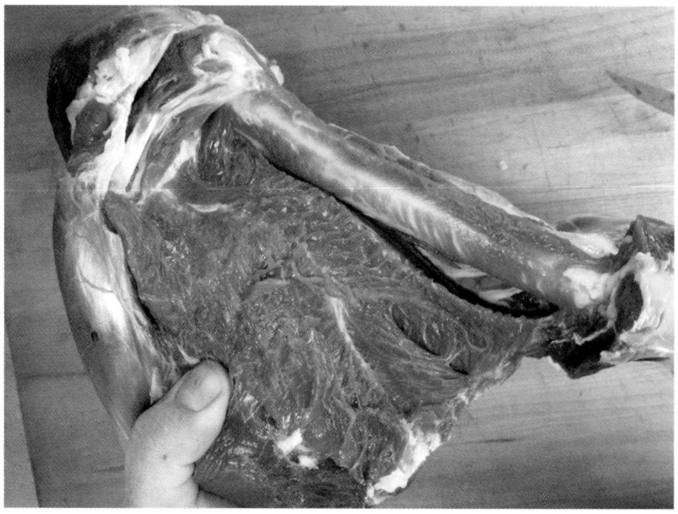

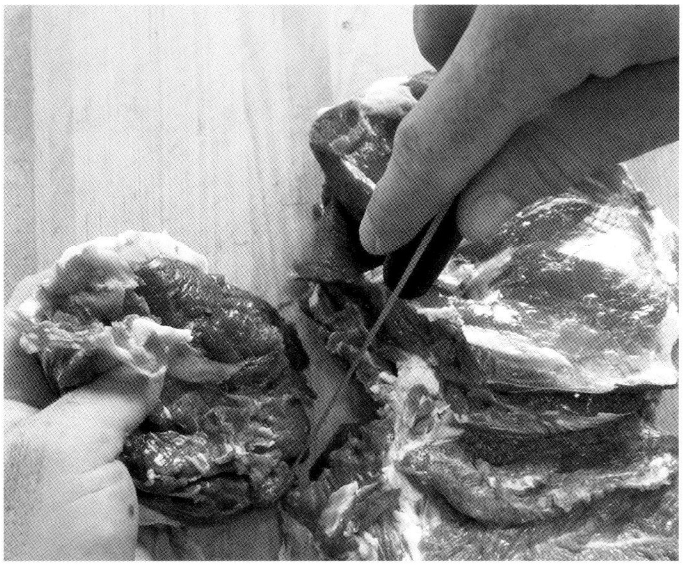

Remove the bone and shank, set aside. Follow all the major muscles and seams. They will guide you on how to cut apart the remainder of the leg: this will give you seven distinct cuts.

From left to right, across the top:
The sirloin tip – braise (cook long and slow with lots of moisture). The heel – grill, sauté and roast. The sirloin – grill, sauté. Scrap – grind into burger.
From left to right, across the bottom:
The top round – thin steaks for the grill, roast, braise. The bottom round with eye attached – remove eye and roast. Grill the bottom round. The shank – braise, stock.

Always remember when cutting sections of the leg into steaks – these muscles are well used on animals that can out run, out jump, out climb the best Olympic athlete. These are not grain fed cows! As such cutting across the grain is vital for a tender section of meat. Does your family enjoy large roasts? If so, think about keeping certain muscles whole and using them as such. My family is not a big "roast" family. So we often make cube steaks out of less tender cuts on the hindquarters.

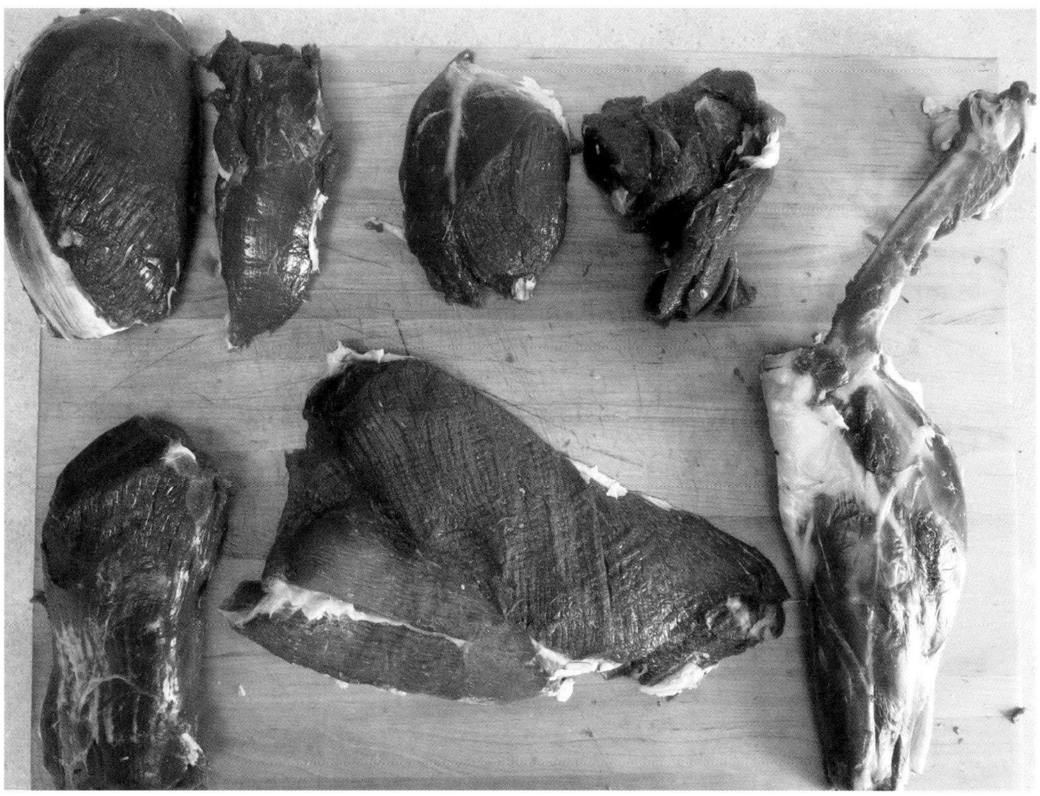

Antelope Solomo

Historically, large sheep populations in Idaho have been managed by Basque immigrants. In fact, Idaho hosts one of the largest Basque populations outside of the Basque homeland. Basque food and culture have been embraced and celebrated by Idahoans for generations. In this spirit, I have adapted a traditional Basque pork dish, solomo, for use with antelope.

Serves 4

1 antelope sirloin
½ cup olive oil
½ cup sweet paprika
¼ cup garlic granules or ¼ cup fresh garlic, chopped
⅛ cup fresh basil, chopped
⅛ cup fresh sage, chopped
Salt and freshly ground pepper, to taste

Mix oil, paprika, garlic, herbs, salt and pepper in a bowl. It should come out as a thick paste. Rub the paste on the sirloin and let sit in refrigerator for no less than 24 hours. Re-apply rub as needed to keep the whole roast covered.

1 onion, sliced
2 red bell peppers, cored, seeded and sliced
20 cloves of garlic, crushed
1 4 oz. jar pimentos
10 green olives, pitted and quartered
1 baguette, sliced and grilled
Fresh cilantro

Olive Aioli

½ cup mayonnaise
¼ cup green and black olives

Preheat oven to 375°F.

Place the onions, garlic, peppers, pimentos and olives in a roasting pan. Place sirloin on top of the onion mix. Roast in the oven until the loin reaches 120°F at the thickest spot.

Mix mayonnaise and olives together in a small bowl. Chill.

Remove roast from oven and it let rest in the pan for about 10 minutes. Slice thin and serve with the onions and peppers, grilled baguette, olive aioli and cilantro.

19

EYES OF A HUNTER

It was mid-April in the high mountain meadows outside Atlanta, Idaho. We set camp at the end of a still impassable logging road and scouted for game. We looked for tracks, for scat, any sign that a bear was in the vicinity.

We were a party of four in the wilderness, getting rain-soaked during bear season. We had been told bears would be waking up and eating the short greens on the snow line. Though we packed miles with our boots and hours with binoculars, we did not see the black shadow of a bear. Like most of my hunting trips, I came home empty handed.

For me, bear hunting always begins the same way; some acquaintance tells me about a bear they watched from afar in a valley somewhere. I go, I hunt around, and I end up without a bear. This has happened enough times that I had started to think of bear hunting as an excuse to go camping in the spring.

Time passed and I had given up on bear for the year – until I went to the birthday party of my son's friend. The black bear rug on the wall invited conversation about hunting bear with the hosts and soon they'd asked me to hunt out of their bait and blind.

In Idaho it is legal to hunt bear over bait: a tagged pile of food, usually in a 55-gallon barrel. In order to run a bear bait a hunter needs to register the bait site with Idaho Fish and Game. Many rules apply as to what can be used as bait.

Bears, like humans, are omnivores and will eat just about anything. Popular baits are things like popcorn and cull onions, really, anything that's sweet. Bear baiting is often an expensive proposition. About twice a week during bear season hunters have to haul up hundreds of pounds of food to keep the bears interested in the site. Gas, time, and the cost of food are prohibitive to all those but the most dedicated hunters.

Luckily, I'd just met such a dedicated new friend.

Like most wild and domestic animals, bears tend to be creatures of habit and fall into a routine when it comes to food. They will hit at specific times of day, most often in the late evening and early morning. It is the hunter's goals to sneak in undetected, and wait for the bear to show up.

Cameras had been placed on the bait site allowing my friend to know about what time the bear typically arrived, usually within a half hour of 9 pm.

The stand was like a well-constructed tree fort – the one you always wanted to build but could never figure out how to make. It was strapped between two trees on the edge of private property outside Horseshoe Bend.

Even with the advantages – the cameras, the bait, the stand – bear hunting is an exercise in patience. I sat in that stand five times, over five different nights, waiting for a bear to show. Conditions must be perfect. Your scent can't overpower his hunger. You can't sneeze at the wrong time. The wind can't blow the wrong direction. Your phone can't beep. Hunting this way has so many uncontrollable factors that tagging out on a bear is far from assured.

On one particularly blustery June day the snow was falling and I was hunting over the bait with my father. I figured that no bear in its right mind would be out and about in that weather. It was going to be another swing and a miss. But after about two hours of playing a game on my phone, strapped to the side of a tree, my father tapped me on the shoulder. A finger to his lips and a grab for his binoculars told me all I needed to know. Bear.

A small cinnamon-colored bear was making his way across the ravine to the bear bait. He was sniffing the air and looked a little nervous. A quick check of the wind showed that my scent was blowing right at him. I had cooked over a stove all day long – I crossed my fingers he'd like the smell of my grease-covered shoes. My heart raced as the bear kept sniffing. I watched as his back legs braced the ground like a dog that's about to bolt. It was time to close the deal, let all this work pay off. Time to shoot.

Make no mistake about hunting: for most of human history, it has kept us alive. It has only been relatively recently that some humans have had enough leisure time away from the procurement of calories and enough distance from nature itself to start questioning the ethics of hunting.

Some, of course, will argue that trail cameras and bait piles provide an unfair advantage to the hunter. Yet, I am a predator without claws, without a nose that can alert me to danger, without eyes that see at night. I need tools to hunt. A bear, on the other hand, is equipped with more evolutionary advantages for staying alive than any number of cameras or amount of bait could ever give a hunter.

Most bear tags issued never get filled. In my hunting life of over twenty years, I have only ever filled one.

Still, others will argue against hunting all together, but a bear is a hunter by nature, as (I strongly believe) am I. We are both predators with incisor teeth and eyes that face forward toward prey.

With those eyes I could see the bear in the scope of my rifle: predator-to-predator. I shot in the only logical place that presented itself, right between his eyes. I pulled the trigger and in the next moment the bear was lying dead across the ravine, about 60 yards away. I didn't even feel the recoil.

Over the next several hours we hauled, eviscerated, and broke the bear down into manageable sections. Quarters, shanks, backstraps, etc. All that was left were the hips, spine and ribs. I grabbed the saw and removed the ribs. I wanted as much of the bear meat as I could get.

To be able to hunt and kill without using the meat goes against every fiber in my body.

Sadly, in Idaho, taking of bear meat is an option for hunters. While the state has wonton waste laws, laws that forbid the wasting of game meat, they do not apply to bear. A hunter can shoot a bear and then leave everything but the skull and hide behind. The skull, still attached to the hide, must be registered with the Idaho Department of Fish and Game. I asked Craig White, a biologist with Fish and Game, to explain the law.

"It is a decision made by the commission," White told me. "We've gone back and forth about it over the years. Bears are not a species that most want to eat, it is a predator…Some areas are very difficult to get in and out of, so we don't ask the hunters to pull the meat out that they might not eat anyway."

White's primary argument is that black bears can sniff out elk calves right after they are born and would attempt to eat the mother and fawn. To keep a base elk population, at levels that can be enjoyed by human hunters, black bears had to be kept at lower than natural levels.

Bear meat must be handled carefully as most bears carry trichinosis, the same parasitic disease that makes moms across the country overcook pork chops and pork roasts. Bears get the disease the way pigs do, by eating other species' trash, trash that contains the round worm *Trichina Spiralis*.

The best way to deal with the trichinosis problem in bears is simple: cook the meat past 137°F. This should kill the bug and your chance of contracting it.

Barbecue Bear Ribs

Sometimes my "Little Chief" smoker just doesn't do the trick, but I can't afford a big fancy smoker either. The solution: turn my barbecue into a smoker. I remove one of the grates and place pre-soaked wood chips in an aluminum foil wrapper right on top of the flame guard. I poke a few holes in the foil so the smoke can escape. I set the barbecue to medium-low only on the side that has the wood chips. When I see smoke I add the meat. I maintain the temperature at about 200°F and let the ribs cook, in the smoke, for 4-5 hours. I rotate the ribs proximity to the heat about every 30 minutes or so. It is amazing how good ribs turn out with a barbecue smoker.

For large wild game ribs I remove the bones from the spine and then cut them again down the middle. The section closest to the spine is the equivalent of "baby back" ribs while the remaining section is considered "St. Louis-style." I treat both sections the same but most pit masters would agree that the St. Louis-style have the most meat and the most flavor.

Serves 2-4

Brine

½ cup brown sugar
¼ cup salt
2 bay leaves
1 cinnamon stick
1 quart of water

Combine the ingredients and bring to a boil in a small saucepan. Remove from heat, cool. Pour the brine over the ribs and marinate for 24-48 hours.

Smoke

Remove the ribs from the brine and pat dry. Place in the barbecue smoker and cook for 4-5 hours at about 200°F. Remove from the smoker and cool.

½ cup barbecue sauce
Freshly ground pepper

Baste the ribs generously with sauce then wrap them tightly in aluminum foil. Bake in a 250°F oven for 1 hour. Remove from the oven, baste again with sauce. The ribs are now ready to eat or they can be cooled and reheated later. I'll pre-make ribs and then refrigerate them so that all I have to do is get them hot at dinnertime.

20

BRINGING HOME THE BACON

I crept as slowly as I could toward the hog. He was about 25 yards away but I wanted to get a little closer for my shot. I stood, unmoving, behind scrub brush and gathered my wits. Breathe, I told myself again and again. 5 yards, all I needed was 5 more yards. Shaking with anticipation, I took slow and steady steps toward the distracted animal. It had been several months since I had harvested a big game animal and my blood was pumping. This was no jack rabbit.

The hog looked in my direction and sniffed the wind. Ruined hunts of the past darted in and out of my mind. The hog turned his head away and I stepped out from the cover of the scrub. I pulled back and shot quickly – too quickly I thought. My arrow flew the 20 yards and struck the hog – a little low and more forward than I would have liked.

He bolted with my arrow sticking out both sides, and then he slowed and finally, dropped. I pulled out my lucky knife, one I'd made years ago out of a sauté pan handle and deer antler. When I rolled the pig over onto his back, thoughts of bacon overwhelmed me. I love bacon.

I have this problem with food: I am obsessed with it. I wake up at night wishing I would have added a little more butter to the sauce – it's a nightmare not to have added enough butter. Fortunately I have channeled this obsession into something useful: I am a chef, and I am a chef that loves bacon. The smokiness, the fattiness, and the I-know-this-is-bad-for-me-but-I-don't-care flavor.

As a chef, one of the best things that I ever learned to do was to make my own bacon. It's a surprisingly easy process that produces outstanding results. The first step is to create a rub recipe. At my house, we are all fans of pepper bacon so I decided that I would come up with a recipe for wild hog pepper bacon.

Concerning the rub, it is important to get the proper ratio of brown sugar to salt ratio so the bacon isn't too salty or too sweet: two parts sugar to one part salt. Beyond that single critical ratio, feel free to experiment with the flavors. I have added things like maple syrup, but only the good stuff out of a glass bottle or star anise for Asian-inspired flavors. Use your imagination.

Step two involves the rubbing and curing of the bacon. The easiest way to cure bacon is to cut it down to a manageable size and place it in large plastic bags. I cut each belly in half width-wise, creating two roughly square-shaped sides of hog belly. With a whole pig I get four pieces. Then I split the bacon rub into four equal parts and rub the mix into the pork belly sections. I am forceful when adding the rub, as increased force ensures penetration into the meat. When the belly sections are covered in rub I transfer them into the bags and seal them. Then I stack the bags and place them in a watertight container, like a big Tupperware or cake pan, in the bottom of the fridge. I advise avoiding the top shelf so as not to accidentally leak raw pig drippings all over the rest of the stuff in the fridge.

Waiting is by far the hardest part of the whole bacon creation process. The minimum amount of time that the belly needs to cure is three days but not longer than five days. Each day I turn and rotate the bellies, making sure each day a new slab of belly is on the bottom of the pile. The pork will release much of its liquid and in turn absorb the rub allowing the flavors to penetrate throughout the belly.

The expunged liquid is called brine and starts to collect after a day or so along the sides of the bag. The brine is good, do not discard it. When rotating the bellies make sure to get the brine all over them. When the cure process is complete you can call the belly by its more noble, rightful, delicious, and sultry name: bacon.

Once the bacon has cured take the bags to the sink, poke a hole in them to drain the brine. Pat the meat dry with paper towels and then transfer it back into the refrigerator on a cookie rack to air dry for one more day. The air drying will create a sticky film on the outside of the bacon that will allow it to absorb more smoke flavor. Do not skip this step.

Now it's time to smoke your bacon. Whatever type of smoker you have, the best bet is to smoke the bacon for at least three hours. If you like more smoke flavor – smoke the bacon a little longer. If you are able to smoke and cook your meats at the same time make sure that you cook the bacon to an internal temperature of 150°F.

My smoker adds smoke and some heat but not enough to cook the bacon. So when I am done smoking, I will transfer the meat to a high-walled cookie sheet and bake it at 350°F for about twenty minutes or until the bacon reaches 150°F at the thickest point. Then I remove the meat from the oven, being mindful of all the fat that has collected at the bottom of the pan. (I don't need another grease burn.)

When the bacon reaches the desired temperature, remove it from the oven and cool to room temperature. As much as I would like to do so, I do not transfer a hot slab of bacon immediately to the refrigerator. When cooled to room temperature, transfer the bacon to the refrigerator and let sit uncovered all night. I suggest that you lock the fridge to prevent slices being cut off by passers-by, including yourself.

When the bacon is fully cooled it is ready to be sliced. If you are fortunate enough to have a mechanical slicer, slice the bacon at a ¼-inch thick, against the grain of the meat. If you do not own a slicer, cutting the bacon with a knife is just fine.

At my house I cut and package my bacon in stacks of twelve slices, enough for everyone in my family to have three pieces of bacon per batch. Then I freeze the stacks. Without preservatives the bacon will not last nearly as long in the fridge as the store bought variety, which is why I freeze what I will not immediately consume.

The preparation methods for making homemade bacon are very similar to store bought bacon, except that the sugar and the herbs can blacken if cooked at too high of a temperature. Otherwise, homemade bacon will crisp up in the final frying, roasting, barbequing, braising or sauté. The biggest difference I notice between homemade bacon and the store bought stuff is that the homemade bacon has actual flavor.

Homemade Bacon

While pig is by far the most common type of bacon, feel free to experiment making bacon from other game bellies. I have made mule deer bacon, elk bacon and wild turkey leg bacon.

Bacon Rub

½ cup kosher salt
1 cup brown sugar
¼ cup freshly ground pepper
3 sprigs fresh rosemary
15 sprigs fresh thyme

Mix salt, sugar, and pepper in a small bowl. Remove the leaves from the rosemary and the thyme stems. The best way is to start at the thinnest part and slide your fingers down to the base of the stem. Then rough cut the herbs and mix with the other ingredients. This should be enough rub for one whole pig belly or two slabs of bacon.

21

LESSONS ON WHITETAIL HUNTING FROM A MULE DEER HUNTER

Truth be told, I have never shot a whitetail in my life. I hunt mule deer, plain and simple. I hunt canyons and sagebrush, juniper trees and some buck brush. Pine trees and I are not the closest of acquaintances. So maybe it's all the *Sportsman's Channel* I watch (or more likely my hubris) that had me convinced I could hunt whitetail deer without a problem. Hell, I've watched Billy Bob and his 6-year-old niece stack whitetail deer up like cord wood, episode after episode. They make it look easy, too easy. With visions of rutting bucks in my head, I walked into the Idaho Department of Fish and Game to trade in my draw tag for an OTC whitetail tag.

Originally I'd put in for a mule deer tag in a special unit, late November, muzzleloader tag – and had actually drawn it for once. The unit is full of logging roads and locked gates, perfect for an uninterrupted hunt. This was supposed to be a great snow filled mule deer hunt with long hikes and big payoffs.

Plans changed when my hunting buddy, and de-facto guide for this hunt, broke his leg falling off a ladder. As excuses go it was pretty legit. I saw X-rays of the fractured femur and the shattered knee cap. His accident was the nail in the coffin on my mule deer hunt. So, I took hope from a different buddy of mine – a guy who had only recently started hunting big game and had scored two whitetail bucks in two years out of northern Idaho, near Riggins. How hard could it be?

For my first whitetail I decided I would take an "easy" route and choose an either sex unit – Unit 33 near Garden Valley, though I had made a pact that I was to going to shoot a doe. Near the town is a vast network of logging roads on public land. It offers clear cuts, farmers' fields and dense pine stands. The valley area is geothermal as well, so big game flocks to the location in winter months for this area free of wolves with considerably less snow.

I chose late October for my first round of whitetail hunting. Unfortunately, I had neglected to notice that it was the opening weekend of elk season. Elk season and whitetail season almost always overlap in Idaho. I saw an orange cap on every ridge, a four-wheeler parked at every gate and not a single deer. The best thing about the whole hunt was watching a herd of elk hide out on a golf course.

Lesson #1 – Whitetail disappear under pressure. Check.

Next I hunted near Riggins, in one of the many creek drainages that surround the Salmon River. As a hunter Riggins will help you define your physical abilities (or disabilities). The country is flat-out steep; most of it pushes 45°. It offers the kind of hiking where you use your hands as much as your feet and you can lean into the ridge by tilting slightly. Again, this hunt presented no luck, not even a white butt in the distance.

Lesson #2 – Just because you hike a lot does not mean you will see whitetail deer.

For my last hunt I went to yet another location. It looked good, out of the truck window, coming back from Riggins. It had clear cuts and was near agriculture. A prime area for whitetail hunting. Or so I thought.

Right at daybreak I arrived at my hunting area, just past New Meadows. I was the first hunter in: the ice on the puddles was unbroken, and I had high hopes. Elk season had just closed so of course the first thing I saw was a nice 5X5 bull at 120 yards, broadside. Next year, I thought.

I crept slowly over ridgelines. I watched the clear-cuts for movement. Eventually I saw movement, at 300 yards: it was a flag-tail. The white butt of a doe came roaring out of the thicket, two yearlings behind her. Of course, I was now hunting a buck only unit. The doe didn't even stop for a second look. I was shocked. How was I supposed to get close to animals that spooked so easy?

Lesson #3 – Whitetail deer have no desire to "hold" like mule deer, they never give you the double look. If you spook them, they are gone.

The rest of the day continued in that fashion – fleeting looks at white asses in the distance. It took me all day to find a place to sit and watch. Poor planning on my end, but now I knew what to do for next time.

Lesson #4 – Know your area, know your deer.

I think this was my fatal mistake; I never hunted the same area more than one time. I always wanted to see new country, always looked for a better spot. My tag sandwich shows the success of this tactic.

I finally figure out why Billy Bob and his niece can stack the deer up. They have a low-pressure private access point. They don't tromp around the woods looking for a buck. They clearly scout the area before and know the deer and their patterns. Here I was thinking that I could just cold-roll into three different locations, have no idea about the deer or their patterns and then find (and shoot!) a buck. I was ashamed of myself. I really want to walk, put on some miles, and earn my meat. But beating brush does not work with whitetail.

Lesson #5 – Act like you are from the East Coast and sit on your butt, for the whole damn day.

This lesson is perhaps the hardest one for me to swallow. I truly do not like sitting while I hunt. It makes me feel lazy.

I never even put crosshairs on an animal that season; the only whitetail buck I saw was on the rack of another hunter's four-wheeler.

Pepper Crusted Venison Steaks

A French classic – peppercorn steak, updated with Northwestern flair. The sweetness of the apples and the apple juice are what make this dish.

Serves 4

6-8 4 oz. venison steaks, sirloin
3 tablespoons cracked black peppercorns
Salt
1 tablespoon olive oil
2 Fuji or Granny Smith apples, peeled, cored and sliced into ¼ inch wedges
1 tablespoon all-purpose flour
¼ cup apple juice (brandy or bourbon works great here, too)
½ cup milk
1 sprig rosemary

Preheat oven to "warm" and place a plate inside.

Pour the cracked peppercorns onto a small plate. Firmly press each of the steaks into the pepper, just one side. Lightly season both sides with salt.

Heat oil in a large heavy-bottomed pan on medium until it is on the verge of smoking. Place the steaks in the pan peppercorn side down and brown for 2-3 minutes.

Flip and cook for an additional 2-3 minutes. Remove promptly from heat if blood starts to show on the top of the pepper-crusted section, this will mean that they are about medium. Place steaks on the plate in the oven to keep warm.

Add the apples and flour to the seasoned pan. The juice from the apples should absorb the flour and not clump. When the apples start to brown add the apple juice, about 1 minute. Use a wooden spoon and scrape the brown bits off the bottom of the pan. The flour should thicken the apple juice mix quickly. Add the milk, let simmer until it reduces and thickens.

Remove steaks from the oven. Pour off any blood from the platter. Slice the meat and serve with the apple sauce, roasted potatoes and sautéed kale. Garnish with rosemary.

Venison Meatloaf

What to do when the freezer is empty of steaks and all that is left is the ground venison? Meatloaf! My momma didn't make much meatloaf growing up but when she did it tasted like this.

Serves 4

3 lbs. ground venison
¼ cup ketchup
2 eggs
1 cup breadcrumbs
¼ cup Worcestershire sauce
2 tablespoons soy sauce
1 tablespoon fresh thyme
2 tablespoons garlic powder
1 tablespoon onion powder
½ red onion, diced
1 carrot, diced
1 cup canned tomatoes, diced and seeded
Tabasco
Salt and pepper
1 lb. of bacon (I prefer Falls Brand, Twin Falls or Hill Meats, Pendleton)

Preheat oven to 350°F.

Mix all the ingredients together, except for the bacon, in a large mixing bowl. Set aside. Line the inside of a bread loaf pan with bacon – two slices should barely overlap on the bottom and drape over the edge of the pan. Repeat until the bottom of the pan is layered in bacon.

Place the reserved meat mixture in the center of the pan and press it into the corners. Fold the bacon over the meat mixture to make a crosshatch pattern over the top. Bake until the internal temperature reaches 135°F. Remove from the oven, tent with foil and let rest for 5 minutes.

Serve with roasted Idaho potatoes.

22

BEST BACKSTRAP EVER

For as long as I can remember, one creature has reigned supreme in my family's diet – the mule deer. I have consumed more mule deer meat than any other wild game animal, by a long shot. Taco meat, hamburgers, meat loaf, stuffed peppers – all using venison. Don't forget the steaks, the roasts and stews.

As such, I fantasize about other deer meat, mostly elk. I have heard that whitetail deer meat is the bee's knees. Can you believe that somehow I have escaped eating whitetail for my whole life? So mythological in its deliciousness has this meat become that I have a fear that eating it will somehow convert me to whitetail exclusively. Never again will I be satisfied with mule deer. This pains me – I am not against sitting in tree stands looking down but I still like spot and stalk hunting!

In the fall of 2012 I was given, as Dr. James Swan puts it the book *In Defense of Hunting*, "the sacrament of wild game meat." My buddy Leon Reams handed me the backstrap from a button buck whitetail he had taken in northern Idaho. He praised the qualities of the meat to me – the tenderness, the flavor. Having never tasted whitetail I argued, feebly, that a young mule deer would taste just as good.

I decided, then and there, that I needed to settle this whitetail vs mule deer edibility discussion for myself.

As a chef that does frequent product demonstrations, I have developed the ability to blind "cut" products against each other with relative ease. However, to properly compare the meats I would a similar piece of mule deer backstrap. Cutting a button buck whitetail against an old and sagebrush fed mule deer would not be a fair comparison. Conveniently, I had recently tagged out on a spike mule deer that was living in my uncle's cornfield.

I had my battling backstraps in the freezer. All I needed was to set up a panel of judges to compare the meat. I figured the panel should be a diverse group of individuals. Hunters, non-hunters, foodies and non-foodies.

First on my list was friend and fellow writer Guy Hand. Guy is the former food critic for the *Idaho Statesman*, a radio show host for a program called *Edible Idaho* and the editor for *Edible Idaho* magazine. Next was Ryan McDaniel, fellow hunter and best man in my wedding. Bowhunter Sean Cook, a backcountry bull buster; Karin Raffo, foodie though wild game novice and Kelly Grindstaff, Executive Chef at Redfish Lake Lodge, rounded out the panel.

Each member of the panel was provided a sheet listing the with a grading scale from 1-10 on the following areas – appearance, color, smell, texture, taste, "game" flavor and overall impression.

The comparison was blind, none of the participants knew if the meat was whitetail or if it was mule deer until the tasting was finished (well, Sean knew the difference. A lifetime of eating both whitetail and mule deer gave it away. He kept quiet about it, however.) The meat was pan roasted in canola oil and seasoned only with salt and pepper. Each loin was cooked to medium rare and served hot, side by side, allowing for direct comparison.

The long and short of it is the whitetail was better. My fear had come true: I could find better meat, although I would have to leave the high desert to get it. I guess it is time to venture into the forest and maybe even sit in a tree stand (I am afraid of heights).

In almost every category the whitetail measured higher than the mule deer. The only time that the mule deer performed better than the whitetail was when it was overcooked.

Category	**Mule Deer**	**Whitetail**
Appearance	8.2	8.2
Color	7.8	8
Smell	6	7.4
Texture	6	9.2
Taste	6.2	9.4
"Game"	6	9
Overall	**6.4**	**9**
Overcooked	5.6	5
Average score	**6.53**	**7.98**

Most notably was the texture comparison between the two meats. We all agreed that the finer grain of the whitetail meant the meat was considerably more tender. The mule deer had longer and tougher strands that Ryan McDaniel noted "are ideal for longer cook times, like braising or stews."

Chef Grindstaff suggested the whitetail was well suited as an "introductory" deer meat something he would be comfortable serving in his restaurant.

Next blind tasting? Elk versus moose. Anyone have any moose meat I could cook?

The Perfect Venison Backstrap

To maintain a tender and juicy backstrap I recommend cooking it like a roast and then slicing instead of cutting the meat into steaks. A large chunk of meat will hold moisture better and is less likely to get overcooked. A single steak can quickly turn into a hockey puck.

Another way to ensure the tenderness of a backstrap is to make sure to completely peel off any silver skin with a sharp tipped knife. Slide the knife directly under the silver skin and then turn the blade up at about a 20° angle; slide the knife under the sliver skin leaving meat behind.

Serves 2-3

12 oz. section of backstrap (whitetail or mule deer)
Kosher salt and freshly ground pepper
1 tablespoon canola oil
Digital or probe meat thermometer

Preheat oven to 350°F.

Rub salt and pepper liberally over the meat.

Heat a medium-sized, ovenproof sauté pan on medium high for about 3 minutes. Add the canola oil – the oil should almost be smoking. Brown the backstrap on all sides. Transfer to the oven and cook until it reaches 115°F at the thickest point.

Remove from the oven and transfer the meat to a warm plate. Let the meat rest for 5 minutes before slicing. A backstrap removed at a rare temperature, 115°F, will finish cooking after a few minutes out of the oven to about 125°F, a perfect medium rare.

Slice the backstrap into ½ inch medallions and serve.

23
ALASKAN DREAM

Alaska almost invariably starts off as a pipe dream. It's on the bucket list, but you're not sure how the hell you are ever going to find enough time or enough money to make it happen. But then you get a bonus at work, you manage to save a little money each month, or you finally declare "to hell with it" and put it on the credit card. Whichever way it happens you find yourself in the far north, actually hunting something, in Alaska, yes, Alaska.

For me Alaska was all about getting what I could not get at home – namely, caribou. I have been dreaming of caribou for as long as I can remember, maybe since the first time I saw Rudolph with his nose so bright. So, when I turned thirty I ran the numbers for a caribou hunt. My dreams came crashing down, all the hunts I could find were prohibitively expensive. I needed a way to hunt without breaking the bank…or causing a divorce.

I vented to my dad and expected nothing more than commiseration. Remarkably, he suggested a "poor man's caribou hunt," something he'd heard about second hand. If you take the Dalton Highway, also known as "the haul road," it'll take you north from Fairbanks and cut right across caribou country. All we had to do was figure out how to get there.

Nine months later I was in a rented camper on the Dalton Highway. My father Larry, and my cousin Jamie, had joined the journey to help defray the costs and shoulder the burden of the equipment. I had used my frequent flyer miles to get to Alaska (thank you day job). Dad and Jamie and I had pre-booked the camper to guarantee the cheapest price. I had scrounged up and shopped on Craigslist for proper backpacking gear. I'd dropped 28 pounds by hiking, running and other conditioning. I could hike 5 miles with 50 pounds on my back in one hour in Idaho. I figured I was ready to rock my Alaska hunt.

Now in order to rifle hunt off the Dalton Highway a person needs to be a least five miles away from the closest point of the pipe. Bow hunting is allowed within five miles but as a traditional bowhunter I know a barren ground caribou is damn near impossible – I am effective to about 25 yards with my recurve.

We parked our truck along the side of the road and then used a three-man raft to ferry across our gear and ourselves. It took seven crossings of the Sagavanirktok River (say that three times fast!) to get everything and everyone across. We stashed the raft in some willows on the other side and walked out along one of the many rivers that run into the Sag.

For a normal person in normal country 5 miles of hiking is not an issue. But the tundra is not normal country. It is wet, ankle-bending country. I liken it to the wettest meadow in early spring, when the dirt is so soft it's a sponge – the water saturates your boots. Every step is hard, like going up a set of stairs but being on flat land.

But it was only 5 miles, right?

Boots we had thought invincible almost immediately became wet through, and heavy. Our packs were crushing, almost aggressively heavy. Did I really need all this damn gear? Our conversation grew darker, everything had seemed all roses and butterflies before the hike out but the reality had set in.

We followed a ridgeline, hoping the higher ground would mean harder ground. We were wrong. We dropped off the ledge and back went down to the river, stopping at about $4\frac{1}{2}$ miles from the pipe.

After we dropped our packs and pitched camp, my dad asked "So… just what the hell are we going to do if you actually shoot one Randy?" We looked at each other, resignation on our faces and I repeated the mantra of the day: "Embrace the suck." If given the option of shooting, I knew I would not hesitate a moment.

After we set up camp I gathered my gear and took off, solo, onto the tundra. Jamie and Dad were too worn out from the hike in to go for another. But I was there to hunt caribou. I could not wait to get 5 miles out and then, finally, be hunting.

My dreams of a great expanse of caribou-filled tundra were dashed. The country was empty, except for a few ducks on the pond. I saw neither hide nor hair of a caribou until I started back to camp at dusk.

When I finally saw some caribou, the setting was picturesque. They were high on a ridgeline, silhouetted by the sun. Big racks were leading the way, heads down and grazing. Their double shovel horns taunted me; clearly they were within the 5-mile corridor. I watched them feed from the willows along a creek bed. Then, much farther down the hill, I saw a solitary bull. I grabbed my GPS – I was 5.07 miles from the pipe.

I crossed out of the brush and paralleled the bull until I was roughly at the same elevation. Only then did he take notice of my presence. I watched him and he watched me. No matter what I did the bull would not let me gain elevation on him. I had him if I wanted to pull the trigger. He was roughly 200 yards out, a chip shot off my shooting sticks.

I checked the GPS again. He was not out far enough. Now he was at only 4.63 miles from the pipe. It was so tempted, I had my crosshairs on that bull, and I wanted, with every inch of my body, to just pull the damn trigger, to end this quest, to get my prize. But I knew I could never feel good about the win, because I would have been cheating the rules. The prize would have meant less.

Plan B: since the bull was not far enough out, I decided I would try and corral him back down the hill and push him out the half-mile. I'd try and get him to cross the creek. Sure, it was a long shot, but what the hell did I have to lose?

But the more I struggled on the tundra, the more the bull just sauntered up the hill. Eventually he raised his tail, and ran off to join the rest of his small bachelor herd. They crested the ridge and disappeared.

Frustrated, I made a line for camp but after only a few steps I noticed movement on the creek bed and quickly pulled my binoculars to my face. Was it a 'bou on the creek? Could I just walk down and shoot one? What I saw took my breath away.

About 50 yards from where I had stopped and glassed the bachelor herd were two grizzly bears. They had busted out of the brush and now were running directly uphill… and straight at me. Although I was a half-mile away from the bears, through my binoculars they were a hellava sight. My innards scrunched up and my testicles lodged in my stomach. I was, just moments ago, right in the path of those bears! In the bushes with two tons of bear. Even worse, it was a mother and her cub. I say cub but this bear was no little thing, it was a two-year-old male and roughly the size of a Volkswagen Beetle. The mother was the size of a

Ford F150.

I instinctively grabbed at my bear spray, and then laughed. No way was this little can of pepper going to stop these beasts. I wasn't going to stick around to prove myself right. I paused long enough to get a few pictures and then get-the-hell-out-of-Dodge before the bears noticed me.

Back in camp I scarfed my wild boar ham and passed out in my tent. I don't even remember lying down. I was spooked and spent. Sleep came easily.

The next morning I awoke before the rest of camp. My Alaska dreams had been renewed – I was caribou hunting and I had just barely missed an opportunity the day before.

I clambered out of bed and woke Jamie and my father. It was coffee and breakfast time. We had slept in, but it was still not fully light. Camp was a bit slow that morning, with ample complaints of sore feet, legs, backs and lack of sleep. Advil went down easy. An airboat buzzed up the river past our camp.

With full bellies and sore legs, Jamie and I set off from camp. Dad was going to hunt near camp, or so he said. I had a sneaking suspicion he was going back to bed when we left.

Again, we had to cover a half-mile of country before we could shoot. I intended to gain a little altitude and look back on the valley from basically the same location that I had spooked the bull. Our hiking was easier than before, no heavy packs this time, but we still stopped for a rest every hundred yards or so. At each stop I positioned my binoculars on my shooting stick as a makeshift monopod.

We made it to the crest of a large bowl and could see the grizzly bear creek below: 5.07 miles from the pipe at its closest point. Anything beyond the creek bed was legal game.

The fog was rolling through in waves, but eventually, on a small finger ridge, I spotted a herd of four animals. "Caribou, holy $#@*!" I instinctively ducked down a little. Not that it would have mattered in the ankle high grass I was standing in. The 'bou were across the creek, legal game, but the herd was making its way toward the river and it seemed as if they intended to cross. That was not something I was going to allow. Jamie and I ran.

With no hesitation we crossed thigh-high water and came up on the opposite side of the creek. We could see the herd more clearly – three cows and a small bull. The bull was leading the herd, slowly feeding toward the river, only 300 yards away.

"I'm shooting the bull, ok? It is the one up front," I said.

"K, I'm shooting the third one back," said Jamie. I counted the herd again; the third one back was a cow. The herd was shuffling.

"You ready?" I mumbled. "Yeah." By now they had spotted us and were giving us the stare down.

"Are you sure you want to kill two?" I asked.

"I'm never going to do this again, so yeah, I'm sure…"

"One, two, three!"

The shooting of guns commenced. The tundra is confusing, the fog is disorienting – we had fallen for the classic optical illusion of tundra hunting. We thought we were in range; roughly 250 yards or so was my guess. It turned out we were about 400 yards from the beasts. I am not a good shot at that range.

Two shots from my gun and I watched my bull buck and stumble. He was hit and was now the third from the front. I watched as Jamie looked down her scope and shot, the bull flinched again. She had just shot my bull…

The bull fell. The three cows walked off, confused and uninjured.

We looked at each other. We both felt victorious, but were wondering why only one 'bou was on the ground. One more shot from my gun, this one from inches away, ended him. He was now no longer an animal; he was a pile of meat.

Upon eviscerating the bull, we could clearly see two distinct caliber sizes in the animal. We had both shot the poor thing. I pulled out my tag and placed it on the horns. The logic was that I had shot the bull more, so I should tag it.

Skinned and quartered, I loaded the bull into my pack – roughly a 110 pounds of meat and bones. Jamie carried out the guns, the head and the heart. All that remained was hide and bones. I trudged until I could see camp and my radio went active.

Over the radio, "How many did you shoot?"

"One bull" I said, dropping my pack and falling to wet ground. I knew help was on the way.

"Good, be right there."

More complaints from Jamie and Dad packing the meat back to camp. I didn't dare whine about it – I was supposed to be the workhorse of this trip, and I knew it. After all, as Dad pointed out, I'd taken a senior citizen and a woman out on the tundra – I'd better expect to do a bunch of the labor.

We hauled the meat back to camp and made a makeshift cooling rack over the cracks in the ground and underbrush. We all agreed that the hunt was over, one 'bou down was enough. As we ate our caribou tenderloin stew, another airboat roared by camp.

Sitting inside a small tepee style tent that was serving as our mess hall, I saw the gears turning in Jamie's head. A smile crept across her face, then a giant grin. "Can I do the dishes?"

Jamie grabbed the pots and the plates and walked over to the water's edge. She didn't scrub a thing but just stood there. I watched her, curious, and waited. I killed time by changing my socks, a practically transcendental experience when out on the tundra.

Jamie waited until she heard the sound of an approaching boat. When the boat rounded a bend in the river, she took to scrubbing the pots in the river. She looked up just as the boat passed by and flashed the driver a wide smile.

I'm not sure what instinct leads men to stop in such situations. Is it sex drive, ego, or perhaps compassion? With just a smile Jamie managed to get that boat to pull over and stop. A short while later the driver was in camp telling stories and listening to Jaime confess our 'plight' in the wild. (I did not hear the first part of the conversation but Jamie later confessed it had something to do with being freezing cold at night and not wanting to sleep on rocks anymore).

Eventually the man offered to give us a ride back to our original river crossing location. No fee, not that he could have charged us anyway according to Alaska law. We did offer him some gas money for his trouble. The man smiled and said he would love to take us back to the confluence – he just needed a little time to go get a few guys at camp and take them back to their truck, then he'd come back up river and grab us. About 2-3 hours he figured. "Get camp ready to go, I'll be back for you," he said, right before roaring off. The man also added that we were the fourth group he "rescued" this season. We let him think whatever he wanted.

After camp was packed we smiled and high-fived each other – we wouldn't have to relive the endless trudge. Jamie and Dad waited by the gear while I fished for grayling. It was the best fishing of the whole trip; I wish I could have enjoyed it more. After all, if the man and the boat did not show back up we had lost a valuable half day of meat hauling, not a good thing.

The man and the boat did show back up and gave us a ride back to our crossing. He unloaded our gear and then went back across the river to get our raft. Our hike out had taken six hours; the boat ride took all of twenty minutes.

"You have steel balls..." he said when I retrieved our raft from the bushes. He shook his head, looking bemused, and tossed the raft on board and stamped out his cigarette in one motion. He was lean, bearded and looked the part of a man who did not screw around; I took that as a compliment.

That night we slept happy and warm in our camper. Part of me felt a little cheated: all the work, the lifting, the running, the hiking with my pack on, the endless hours sweating my butt off and in the end I'd spent a total of one night out on the tundra. I had come to Alaska in search of caribou and shot one on the second day of trying. I had lived the dream, but I wanted it to last longer. I wanted to linger in the moment, to savor it.

But things needed to be done. Time to gas up; ship the meat home, round up some souvenirs, fish a little more. My Alaskan dream was complete.

I hear that moose hunting in Alaska is fun. Looks like I need to start saving.

Pan Roasted Caribou Steak with Watermelon, Corn and Zucchini Salad and Brown Butter Sage Vinaigrette

This recipe uses fall flavors on summer ingredients, to a surprising affect in my opinion. Butter and sage, staples for butternut squash and halibut are added to watermelon and zucchini. It is a combination of sweet and savory that works great. Feel free to kick it up a notch with a little red chili flake. Then you have a trifecta of flavor – sweet, heat and savory.

Serves 4

Brown Butter and Sage Vinaigrette

¼ cup unsalted butter
20 fresh sage leaves
1 garlic clove, crushed
¼ cup Balsamic vinegar
½ cup canola oil
¼ cup Parmesan cheese, grated
Salt and freshly ground pepper

Melt butter in a medium-sized sauté pan. Add the sage and turn heat to medium high, the pan will spit a little oil out on you. Be careful. Watch the butter closely; it should turn brown in about a minute. Add the crushed garlic when the butter is brown in color and has a nutty smell. Add the vinegar and the canola oil to the hot pan. This will cause some aggressive boiling, do NOT inhale the fumes. Add Parmesan to the pan and remove from heat.

Puree vinaigrette in a blender or food processor until smooth. Season to taste. Reserve at room temperature.

Caribou Steak

2 caribou steaks, about 8 oz. each
Salt and freshly ground pepper
1 tablespoon butter
1 small zucchini, cut into large cubes
1½ cups cubed watermelon
1 ear of corn, removed from cob
2 cups lambs quarters, or spinach

Rinse and wipe out the same pan you made the vinaigrette in. Season the venison steaks with salt and pepper. Melt the butter over medium heat. When butter is melted but not yet brown add the steaks to the pan. Cook until dark brown on one side, then flip over and cook until

blood begins to rise to the surface of the steak. The steak temperature will be about medium rare.

Remove the meat and add the zucchini. Cook until golden on one side, flip. Toss in the watermelon and corn. Warm for 1 minute.

Place the lambs quarter or spinach in a medium salad bowl. Dress with 3 tablespoons of vinaigrette. Toss vegetables and watermelon with greens.

Slice the steak. Pile the salad on a plate, place the steak on the top.

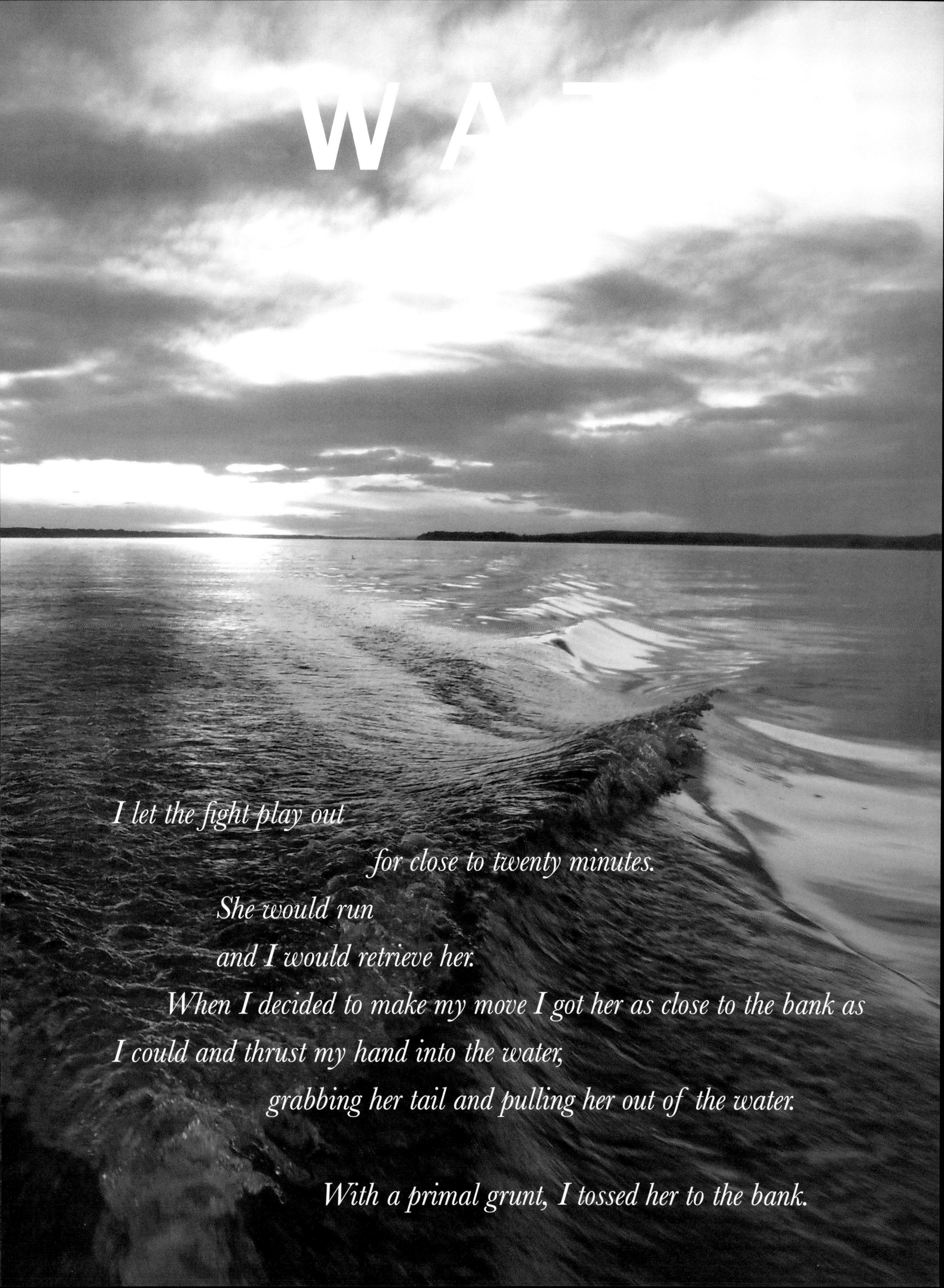

WAT

I let the fight play out
for close to twenty minutes.
She would run
and I would retrieve her.
When I decided to make my move I got her as close to the bank as I could and thrust my hand into the water,
grabbing her tail and pulling her out of the water.

With a primal grunt, I tossed her to the bank.

24

EAT THE CARP

The banks of the Snake River are not a hospitable place, but there I was, squeezing my way to the water in search of an invasive species – not a hog, deer or other animal but the lowly and oft-mocked carp. The plan was for me to shoot it with my bow.

The carp is not native to the water of Idaho. Introduced in the 1880s as a protein resource, the humble carp was a big let down to the United States Fish Commission, a precursor to Fish and Game. The hope was that aquaculture, carp especially, would become as "important among the American Farmers and planters as the cultivation of cattle, sheep, swine, poultry or of grains, fruits and berries."

The Fish Commission got it wrong: aquaculture of carp is almost nonexistent in America. Even Idaho, home to a very productive aquaculture center just south of Boise, does not farm carp. They just never caught on as an edible fish when compared to trout, bass or catfish.

Nonetheless these fish lurk in our waters and some have taken up arms, literally, against them. The leader of the pack in Idaho is Brian Pokorney, a chapter representative of the Idaho Bow Fishing Association.

According to Porkorney, "Bow fishing is a sport that involves using a bow, whether it is a compound, recurve, long bow, or a crossbow with a reel attached holding a special type of line that is attached to a fiberglass arrow…It's a form of hunting that has been used for ages as a way to acquire food." The goal of bow fishing is to shoot into the water with a fiberglass arrow, hit the carp and then reel it in with a string that is attached to your arrow. While it might technically be a form of hunting, all you need to have in Idaho is a valid fishing license to shoot non-game species of fish like the carp.

"Carp can have an adverse effect on a whole fishery as they feed on the eggs of game fish and reduce the amount of food for them. They reproduce in huge numbers and can take over a body of water if they are not controlled," said Pokorney.

According to Dave Parish, from Idaho Fish and Game, "Carp like the shallow areas, they root around in the mud and this affects water quality. That impact is hard on the native fish populations because it inhibits the growth of phytoplankton and zooplankton. They basically affect the whole food chain in a river."

The carp is a prolific springtime spawner in the shallow waters along riverbanks and reservoir shores. And it's at this time when most bow fishermen strike. "During this time of year [carp] are cruising the shore lines and are swimming shallower than normal making them more visible," and consequently easier to shoot, according to Jeff Fealko, the chapter president of Idaho Traditional Bowhunters.

According to Fealko, "On a good day you would be able to feed an entire block; you can easily shoot up to a dozen carp in a few hours" But do bow fisherman really eat this much carp?

"I don't eat the carp and I never have, it's my understanding that because they have many bones and with their diet they are not very edible," said Pokorney. "We have people that take the carp for animal food as well as fertilizer uses, sometimes we just bury them to dispose of them. We don't ever put them back in the water to rot."

Said Fealko: "Many people eat whatever they shoot and I should try carp at some point, but currently I do not eat the carp I shoot…A lot of the time I will try to find a local farmer that will plow the carp under their fields for fertilizers, otherwise I recycle them for bear bait."

As I pressed closer to the waters of the Snake River, sneaking from rock to rock, I spotted a carp cresting. 15 yards from the bank below the Swan Falls Dam I pulled my bow back and shot. An arrow flies strangely with the string attached to it and I watched as it plummeted into the water about two inches in front of the fish. The arrow didn't sink, instead the arrow, and the fish, swam rapidly upstream nearly tugging by bow from my hand. I wrapped string around the primitive reel attached to my bow. The fight was on – the more I tugged the harder the fish swam. Slowly the carp came closer to the shore. It was nearly in hand when the arrow came loose from his skin and the carp started flopping its way back to the water. I grabbed the fish by the tail and hoisted my 10-pound trophy into the air.

Back at camp, I gutted the fish and filled it full of onions. I wrapped it in foil and tossed it into the fire. Thirty minutes later, I was having a hard time convincing the rest of camp to eat the fish; it was a carp after all. The cat fishing poles were in the water and that was the real goal.

I have eaten carp a number of times. It is not a bad tasting fish but it does lack in the texture department. They are a little soft on the bite, kind of like pollock. The rumors that carp are full of bones are entirely true. The fish is riddled with them. The best bet for avoiding the bones is proper filleting.

As far as I can tell most bow fishermen are like me, not exclusively bow fishermen. Most are bowhunters and fishermen who like to have a good time and get rid of a pest at the same time. As Fealko put it to me, "Hour for hour spent on the water, I don't know if I have done any fishing that is as fun and entertaining as bow fishing. Watching an arrow arc through the air and into the water at a 20 pound carp is priceless, especially when you connect."

25

CITY FOLK STEELHEAD

Generally, fishing is not a spot and stalk sport for me. My standard method for fishing is to toss a line into the deep and hope for the best. But steelheading on the Boise River, right in downtown Boise, is a different story.

During my lunch break, I take the five-minute walk to a dock right on the river at Barber Park. I watch a white-headed steelhead swim slowly in the shallows – she is big and she is ugly. The fish was suffering from what is called Ulcerative Dermal Necrosis, basically ulcers on her head from being beaten up in the shallow river for so long. It is a common occurrence during the spawning season. As soon as I walk close to the edge she would swim into the current and disappear, sometimes other smaller steelheads would swim off as well.

I cast and cast at the riffle and the pool above it, hoping to get a strike from a silver slime rocket. Most days I was disappointed and simply cast for practice, but not on Friday, November 30th. I snuck out with my ultra-light trout rod with 6 pound test and a copper "Big Deal" lure. I crept out on the dock and saw my ugly headed foe. She saw me, too, and bolted, but only to the edge of the current. I sent my cast about six feet in front of her ulcered head and slowly reeled in, right to her face. With her one good eye she struck my lure. I felt a bump but no run; but I could see my lure in her mouth. I did the only logical thing and set the hook as hard as I possibly could. Oh, how I wished I had brought a bigger fishing pole.

With my rod bent in half and no net I realized the problem. I was about four feet above the water and could not possibly land the fish I never thought I would catch. I had to jump off the landing and into the rocks beside it, never mind that I was in slacks and chefs clogs.

The hum of my drag was nearly constant as I fought the big gal. I would reel her close to the bank and as soon as she spotted me she would bolt (she really did only have one good eye). I let the fight play out for close to twenty minutes. She would run and I would retrieve her. When I decided to make my move I got her as close to the bank as I could and thrust my hand into the water, grabbing her tail and pulling her out of the water. With a primal grunt I tossed her to the bank.

I hooted and hollered and danced on the bank looking at my 30-inch nine-pound steelhead. My endorphin rush lasted just long enough for me to ignore the other feeling I was having, hunger.

While it might seem like blind luck that I caught that fish, I was actually approaching the river with a little bit of expertise.

Us litter river fishermen all want to be on the big rivers, the Columbia, the Snake, the Clearwater, catching some lunkers. Instead we're stuck in the Boise valley. Fortunately, Fish and Game stocks the Boise River each year with hatchery born steelhead from the Oxbow Dam. The steelhead run up to the hatchery and are loaded onto a truck and hauled to Boise. Fishermen can actually catch steelhead while ESPN broadcasts from the Smurf turf at the Boise State Stadium (Go Broncos!).

Each year the fish dump creates a little microclimate for fishermen. Hundreds of people congregate across the four drop locations trying to land a steelhead.

The small water of the Boise River requires a specific tactic. Instead of jigging for fish at 6 feet you jig for them at 2 feet. Diver-style plugs are out of the question. The best bet for landing an "in town" steelhead is what local fishermen Kelly Chatterton calls a BSA: "Big, Silver and Annoying."

Spinners and spoons tend to dominate the fishing action in the Boise River. Specifically, the Blue Fox Super Vibrax in silver. "Basically, it is the job of the fisherman to knock the big boys on the head with a lure and make them strike it…the strike is out of anger, not hunger," added Chatterton. Others use bait right after the fish are dumped.

When the water is low sight fishing is not uncommon. Often the fish can be seen at mid-day, at the edges of holes. Not spooking the fish is crucial to successful sight fishing on the Boise. Cast above the fish and try and get the lure as close as possible to the head, which will hopefully induce a strike.

In general, fishing is best right after the fish are deposited. They tend to be confused and have not settled into the river, that and there are a lot more fish per mile of water.

How to get more meat off a steelhead

Protein recovery becomes an issue when you get your big fish to shore. We all want to be as respectful as possible of the life that we have taken, but many of us lack the skills to harvest the meat in the proper way. No worries. I have a little trick that will make you feel good about your fillets, even if they are not perfect.

When the fish is done being filleted, most people will simple toss the bodies. However, a large amount of meat, often as much as a pound, may be left on the skeleton. Simply scrape down the side of the fishes exposed sections with a spoon, removing the flesh. Scrape the backbone clean of most of the meat. Pile this meat up and reserve for fish taco night, for sandwiches or pasta. No need to crumble up the perfect fillets when you have crumbled meat already.

Almond Crusted Steelhead with Chilean Barbacoa Sauce and Fingerling Potatoes

Serves 2

Fingerling Potatoes

½ pound mixed fingerling potatoes, quartered
1 small carrot, shredded
½ cup edamame or frozen peas
1 tablespoon butter
10 mint leaves, thinly sliced
Salt and freshly ground pepper

Heat oven to 325°F. Melt half the butter in a medium sauté pan. When the butter is foaming add the potatoes and toss to coat. Place in oven and bake for 15 minutes or until fork tender. Add the carrots, peas, butter and mint leaves. Toss and season with salt and pepper. Cover with lid and reserve, the residual heat will finish the peas and carrots.

Chilean Barbacoa Sauce

This sauce is from Kelly Chatterton, a steelheader and chef from Boise. Kelly likes this sauce for big ocean run brown trout from Chile.

½ cup brown sugar
1 tablespoon soy sauce
1 tablespoon Worcestershire sauce
3 tablespoons Dijon mustard
1 tablespoon garlic powder
½ cup port, sherry or Madeira
½ cup sherry vinegar
3 tablespoons tomato paste

Combine ingredients in a small saucepan. Heat to a boil and remove from heat. Reserve.

Almond Crusted Steelhead

½ cup almonds, sliced and crushed
2 6 oz. steelhead fillets
1 tablespoon canola oil
Salt and freshly ground pepper

Preheat oven to 325°F.

Wet the fish slightly under the tap. Massage the almonds onto the inside surface of the fish (not the skin side). Place skin side down. Heat oil in a medium sauté pan. Place fish almond side down into the pan, cook for 2-3 minutes or until the almonds are toasted. Flip and move pan to oven. Cook for about 5 minutes or until fish is done.

Place half the potatoes and one of the fillets on a plate. Garnish with 2 tablespoons of sauce.

26

THE $50 CRAPPIE

The sun is out and my flesh is starting to burn. The warming weather has turned me into a special kind of fiend: a lobster-skinned, overly-optimistic crappie fisherman. For some reason these diminutive little fish, and their cousins bluegill, have caught my eye. I find myself sitting in my cheap green boat (appropriately named the SS Money Pit) tossing jig after jig with nary a bite.

I am told that the Owyhee Reservoir in Eastern Oregon is the place to be. I have been lured by tall tales of bucket after bucket of crappie being pulled out of the water. Rumor has it they strike at whatever moves as long as it is in the right place. As the water warms, the stories move closer and closer to land; by mid-summer bank fishermen are landing stringers full.

I've got my out-of-state one-day license, my invasive species sticker, gas for the boat, registration for the boat and all the other ancillary materials needed for an inaugural boat launch. Then, I fish my heart out for a solid four hours with not a single bite.

I use every technique I can think of to catch a fish, starting with the bobber and the worm. Some days they work wonders. Find the depth of the fish and they will strike. Not today. Then I tried a bobber, jig and worm combination. Again, adjusting my depth. No bites. Then, in a magic moment, a tug at the end of my line calls me. I set the hook and land a hand-sized crappie on the "drop shot" jig technique. Drop shotting is when you attach the hook a foot to a foot and a half up from the bottom of the line and then attach split shot on the end. The idea is that the split shot bounces along the bottom and elevates the jig off the bottom and into striking depth.

Like most poor people, I have to play the game of "guess that noise" with my vehicles. On the way to another location the engine of the SS Money Pit started to make a terrible rattle. Something in the pull start housing had come apart. Afraid to stop the engine, we might not get it going again, we rolled back to the dock. I only caught the one fish that day. With all my investment, I figure it was at least a $50 crappie.

I learned about drop shotting from an old man sitting at a dock in Caldwell. I was casting my small jig over and over. I noticed he would simply cast and very slowly retrieve; he caught fish, I did not. That day I learned to find the old man.

Look for a retirement-aged gentleman who has the leathery skin of a fisherman (and avid housework avoider). These guys know the water, the fish and the technique. Sometimes they are helpful. Even when they are not, I take my cues by spying.

I have been hitting the local ponds, too. Some hold remarkably large pan fish populations. That said, urban stocked ponds often house smallish fish that are hard to justify keeping. I find that these ponds are great for kids – when the pan fish are spawning they are hard to keep off the line.

According to pond management folks, overpopulations occur when a lack of predation is present. Fishermen catch all the bass and the bluegill population explodes. This is a problem in many urban ponds in Idaho. Large numbers of fish in a pond mean the fish are competing over food and can't eat themselves any bigger than 4-5 inches. Catching a normal-sized crappie or bluegill can seem like a trophy. That's why, in my opinion, the bass in urban ponds should almost always be returned to the water.

I am a "catch and eat" type of guy but a little bass management, in the form of returning them to the pond, is a good thing.

When looking for a lunker pan fish, search in hard-to-access areas. I routinely pull out larger bluegill just by hopping into a raft and paddling to a less accessible part of a local pond. A float tube and a fly rod is huge fun, too. Toss a jig on a weighted line and watch the magic happen.

Fried Crappie with Orange Pineapple Salsa

Let's face it; the yield on pan fish is low. I almost feel bad when I fillet a crappie or a big bluegill. You take the tough fighting little fish out of the water and end up with barely any meat. To increase yield I scrape the spine with a spoon for extra meat, on a big batch of fish this can lead to a whole extra meal for my family: I use the scrape for ceviche or fish tacos or a crappie salad sandwich.

YouTube has lots of really good videos on how to fillet pan fish. It's fairly easy and when you get the hang of it you'll be able to process the fish very quickly.

Serves 2

Orange and Pineapple Salsa

1 large orange, cut into segments
¼ pineapple, peeled and diced
Salt and freshly ground pepper
1 tablespoon hot sauce, such as Chipotle Tabasco or Cholula

Cut about ½-inch off the top and bottom off the orange. Stand the orange on one of the flat sides and peel using a knife, making sure to remove a little bit of the orange flesh. The goal is to remove the bitter white section closest to the skin of the orange. Segment with a knife. Toss the citrus with the hot sauce. Salt and pepper to taste. Refrigerate.

Fried Crappie

10 crappie fillets, scaled
4 cups canola oil
¼ cup flour
¼ cup corn starch
1 teaspoon garlic powder
1 teaspoon salt
1 teaspoon freshly ground pepper

In a Dutch oven or other heavy pan, heat the oil over medium heat to 350°F. Don't let the oil smoke.

Lightly flour a dinner plate, set aside. Mix the flour, garlic powder, salt and pepper in a gallon-sized zip-top baggie. Wet the fish a little under the sink. Then add the fillets, one at a time, to the bag. Shake the bag to coat the fish evenly. Transfer the fillets to the floured plate.

Slide each fillet into the hot oil very carefully. Fry for 2-3 minutes or until golden brown. Remove and drain on a paper-towel-lined plate.

Serve with salsa.

27

HALF-SHELL BASS

I vividly remember my ex-girlfriend's house – not for any of the reasons you might be thinking – but because her dad was a semi-pro bass fisherman. The basement was a trove of lures, plastics, rods, reels and nets. It was like being at a sporting goods store, but organized by a crazed and over-protective lumberjack. All he talked about was the last and/or next tournament. How he bounced the jig off this rock or how he wacky-hooked a chartreuse (what color is that anyway?) worm over the lily pads. The man had one of those low-slung, ridiculously fast boats that look like they've been painted with sparkly red nail polish. He had the big truck to pull the boat, too.

The man was a "catch and release only" type of guy. I was all about keeping and eating fish. So, clearly, he and I did not see eye to eye. The fact that I was dating his daughter probably didn't help either. It was all rather intimidating. I took verbal lessons on how to fish from our conversations, but I always kept a secret weapon in my arsenal. Worms.

That's right a good old *Lumbricus terrestris* – the earthworm. Believe it or not, these garden dwellers are not native to the Americas. They are, technically speaking, an invasive species. During the last ice age, the weight and cold of the glaciers that topped most of the United States killed off ground worms. They came back in force with European settlement. In fact, sections of this country are still "earthworm free" zones and to protect localized ecosystems they have banned worms as bait.

I vividly remember catching a dozen plus fish without moving off a single rock in the Snake River. The water formed a back eddy on the other side of a flat boulder. All I had to do was drop my line into the hole and the fish would hammer my line. I watched as my girlfriend's dad changed color after color, pattern after pattern, top water to crayfish plastics all without landing a single fish. I smiled a lot and could not keep my little mouth shut. My worm fishing made me a heretic and unfit for his daughter to be near (that or something about a late night drop-off and big black Ford, but I digress).

Fast forward twenty years and I am in possession of a cheap ass aluminum boat that is mostly good for duck hunting and lake cruises. Not being a semi-pro bass man, I feel no need to have a fiberglass water ride that is more expensive than my daily driver. And I still fish with worms, one of the single best options for catching a bass.

Bass are carnivores and will eat just about anything that swims by which keeps lure manufacturers in business. Seriously, what the hell are some of those top water lures supposed to be? I saw one the other day that was just a white floating tube with hooks on it. A little worm wiggling around on the hook is the real deal: food for fish.

I set up multiple riggings for my pole – most derived from the drop shot technique. Drop shotting is when the weight is at the end of the terminal tackle and the hook, or hooks, is located up the line a few feet. I have, with great success, used a regular old bait hook with a worm and a soft plastic combination. Tossing that split mix into cover, more than half the time the worm is struck before the plastic.

The one-two punch of plastic and bait catches a variety of fish. It is a hellava good time to catch a big ole catfish on a bass rod. Chances for that go up exponentially with a little meat on the hook bobbing around.

Another added bonus of worm fishing is that you can be lazy. The movement and the smell coming off the little hunk of protein attract the bite, so you don't always have to be reeling. This allows for more beer drinking and conversation.

Worms catch fish and if catching fish is the goal, then there is no good reason not to use them. Screw the purists.

If you're going to eat your catch, and you should, eat the ones that are barely legal. Why? The bigger fish tend to be the spawners – they maintain the population. Also, many of the rivers and ponds that are home to bass are "working systems." Basically that means that the farms dump into them. Dairy's too, sewer plants even. As predatory fish bass accumulate the nasty bits and chemicals over time – think mercury. Eating the smallish ones means that they are not full of junk, typically. Same story with catfish, too. Abide by the "only eat one per week" and the "not for pregnant women and children" signs, too.

Grilled Smallmouth Bass "Half Shell" with Preserved Lemons and Peas

There's no two ways about it: scaling fish sucks. I am not a fan, and neither is my wife. There is almost always a scale or ten scattered and glued to the appliances when I clean up afterwards. So, I figured out a way to be a lazy fish cook: the "half shell" method. Simply cut off the side of the fish and leave the scales intact. Make your first cut directly behind the gills and past the pectoral fins. Then slide your blade along the backbone, removing the side. The scales form a guard and protect the soft white fish of the bass keeping it moist and tender. On several occasions I have tested the theory with skeptical friends. Every time the fish with the scales left attached was juicier and more flavorful.

This recipe calls for preserved lemon, which is a classic North African preparation that preserves the lemon by packing it in salt. Preserved lemons are tart but not overly so and work in all places that a normal lemon would; they are just more interesting. You can find them at specialty groceries or make your own *(see recipe page 163)*

Serves 4

2 "keeper" bass
Salt and freshly ground pepper
1 preserved or regular lemon – cut in half
1 cup sugar snap peas, halved
1 cup pea shoots
1 roasted red pepper, julienned
1 tablespoon Balsamic vinegar
1 tablespoon olive oil
1/4 cup grated Parmesan cheese

Heat grill to medium. Place the fish, scale side down, on the hot grill. Season with salt and pepper. Smear half the preserved lemon along the sides of the bass. This will impart a lemony flavor during cooking. Cover the fish or close the lid of the barbecue, cook for about 5 minutes or until the fish is flaky. The time it takes will depend on the thickness of the bass.

In a small mixing bowl add the peas, pea shoots, red peppers, vinegar, oil and cheese. Cut and remove the flesh – leaving the pith and rind – of the remaining lemon. Cut the rind into very thin strips, (the zest from a fresh lemon works, too).

Toss together and season with salt and pepper.

28

IDAHO KITTY FISH

The anchor was out on the small flat-bottomed boat that belonged to Ryan Scott. I let it loose in about 5 feet of water and we drifted slowly downriver until the big weight found a solid hold on the soft river bottom. I looked at the fish finder and saw that we had drifted to the edge of a hole in the river – a section carved by two river currents colliding. It was three-times deeper than the normal stretch of river – and it had gobs of fish floating in it. We cast into the wide expanse of the Snake River laid out before us. On one side were farmers' fields; the other side was a stellar view of Idaho wine country. But this wasn't a dainty wine sipping adventure. No, I was after the mighty and oft-overlooked catfish.

It is a rite of passage for many an Idaho boy to sit around a fire along the Snake River and hope that a kitty fish tugs on the end of his line. But the drunken exploits of amateurs have ruined the reputation of this sport for others.

You see, fly fishers stalk pan-sized fish like deer in the small mountain streams and bass fishermen cast lures into reeds and muck in hopes of a tug. Casting and casting over and over again. Work, work, work. All in the hope they might land a fish that is just a few pounds in weight.

In contrast, cat fishermen primarily use bait: worm, rotten chicken liver or dead fish. They cast and let the fish come to them. Big fish, too. On good nights on the Snake River, if you are positioned well, you can pull in 20 to 30 fish ranging from 5 to 18 pounds each. If you get lucky, you can even haul in a sturgeon.

Trout and bass fishermen call cat fishers lazy and undisciplined. But not Scott. He is a man with a passion for catching big fish, no little pan fry is enough for him – a 4-pound bass is a bonus but an 18-pound catfish is a prize.

The cats Scott catches are not from around these parts. According to Jeff Dillon, the state fisheries manager for the Idaho Department of Fish and Game, "There is no native cat-fish west of the Rockies." So all that perfect habitat, the calm waters of the Snake River, was catfish-less until someone in the mid 1800s got the bright idea to introduce them to the river and badabing badaboom: catfish in the West.

I relayed that tidbit of information to Scott and then explained that Idaho doesn't have any blue catfish, either.

"That is a bunch of bull." He cocked his head and pulled out his phone. "Here is a picture of one." He pointed, "We caught him off that island about a mile up river." I informed him that according to Dillon at Fish and Game, no blue cat has ever been reported in Idaho. I looked at his photo, sure enough, it was a blue cat as far as I could tell.

Although we could see plenty of fish in the hole, more than an hour passed without a bite. The water temperature was 77°F and it was getting dark so we moved on. We traveled slowly downriver, passing over spots that only registered 1½ feet deep.

I questioned Scott as we floated along about the discrepancy between his fancy fish finder and his boat.

"What I got here," said Scott "is $2,000 worth of rims on $1,000 car. It don't make much sense but this little boat can go further into the muck and shallows than any of those bigger boats, and that's how I get on the big fish."

Catfish do get big in Idaho. According the Idaho Fish and Game website, the state record channel catfish, the kind that Scott catches most of the time, was more than 38 pounds. The record flathead catfish was 58.5 pounds, with a girth of 31 inches. The head of a fish that big wouldn't even fit in a 5-gallon bucket.

Eating a fish that large, however, comes with a cautionary warning. Recently the Idaho Center for Disease Control released a statement advising the limited consumption of catfish caught on the lower Boise River because of higher-than-normal levels of mercury.

Catfish are predators and eating other contaminated fish increases their own contamination levels. Therefore the CDC recommends eating smaller catfish and cutting away the skin and fat before eating them.

Scott and I fished for a long time that night; it was actually early (as in morning), before we landed a fish. Then came the slightest of tugs on the line followed by a rod-bending pull. I grabbed my rod and set the hook; the fight was on. Five minutes later, I had a 6-pound catfish in the boat.

We hung out for thirty minutes more and landed an additional 4-pounder for the freezer. Cat fishing may not be as highly regarded as fly or bass fishing, but even small cats like the two I caught with Scott can ruin a guy on trout and bass. Just because these are Idaho catfish doesn't mean I can't make a good old-fashioned po-boy out of them. Well, "old fashioned" might be the wrong choice of words. The recipe that follows is for a Northwest-style po'boy – rustic bread, farmstead pickles, and Asian spicy cabbage slaw with blueberry vinegar. Some will call this sacrilege; I call it "regionalization."

Fried Catfish Po'Boy

I have refused to buy one of those little baby deep fryers for my house over the years out of concern for my health. I LOVE fried food and as a chef eat plenty of it at work. If given the opportunity at home I know I would consume even more fried goodness (bumping me a few pant sizes at the same time). To counter the "no fryer" rule I just make a more dangerous version in a cast iron skillet. Smart? No.

I like to use a good grainy hoagie roll for this sandwich but the traditional white/sourdough varieties work, too.

Serves 4

1 lb. catfish fillet, cut into 2- inch strips
1 cup milk
1 large egg
1 cup yellow cornmeal
½ cup all-purpose flour
2 cups canola oil
Pinch cayenne pepper
1 tablespoon freshly ground pepper

Soak the catfish in milk for 15 minutes or up to 24 hours (some claim that this will "lessen" the mud flavor of the fish, I'm not exactly sure…I've never tested it). Beat egg in a small bowl until frothy. In a separate bowl, mix together cornmeal, flour, cayenne and pepper. Dip fish strips into the cornmeal mixture a few pieces at a time. Set them on a plate in a single layer. Dip them in the egg and then back into the cornmeal, pressing the fish into the dry mix so they are extra coated. Repeat until all the fish is double-dipped.

Heat oil in a skillet to 350°F. Fry strips for 3-4 minutes until they are crispy and cooked.

Slaw

½ head of green cabbage, shredded
1 carrot, peeled and shredded
¼ cup buttermilk dressing
1 tablespoon blueberry vinegar (huckleberry is better if you can get it)
1 tablespoon honey
1 tablespoon Sriracha
Salt and freshly ground pepper

In a small bowl combine the dressing, vinegar, honey and Sriracha. Next add the cabbage and carrots, toss until coated. Salt and pepper to taste.

Split the hoagie rolls and toast. Add the fish and top with the slaw. Add some pickles that your newly gardening neighbor gave you and you got a grubbin' po'boy.

PILOT

29

RIPPED LIPS AND SEASICK

Eighteen miles out into the Pacific Ocean the boat came to a stop. Well, kind of a stop. The 10 foot waves continued to rock the boat while the 16-year-old deck hand, aptly named Noah, came into the cabin and announced that we were tuning the boat around due to weather conditions.

I heard a sigh come from the passengers but I couldn't tell if they considered it bad news. It was not bad news to me. I was sitting with my head down in the cabin trying to keep my insides inside. The ride had been so rough that I counted myself as one of nine people on board, out of twelve, who had chummed the water that morning. My face turned a shade of green; I had only ever heard of this happening, never had I seen it on my own face. I had watched a boat full of optimistic and enthusiastic fishermen and women turn into a zombie-faced band of mutineers.

Sure, I got to see a whale surface. A big grey came up through the waves and crashed down into the water. Part of me thought it was the coolest thing I had ever seen, the other part of me wanted nothing more than a section of dry land to call my home, to make a small garden and retire on, never to see the ocean again. That is the land lover in me.

I sat with the other deck hand, Steven, on the way back and tried to make conversation. Honestly, I was just trying to keep my mind off the rocking of the boat. We chatted about football, hunting and, of course, the sea. "We want to catch fish you see," Steven said. "It is in our blood. We can't pull into port at 9 am, bad things, catastrophic things happen when we do; fishermen love two things – the sea and our booze."

"When we go out and Captain Carl doesn't think we are gonna catch fish no one questions his decision to turn around…They call him the Son of Neptune," Steven added, "I swear fish recognize the underside of his boat and flock to it. Captain Carl is the man. I've wanted to fish with him for years…everyone wants to fish with him." These words hung on the room thickly, like an especially effective Super Bowl commercial. His leather-like face had seen a lot of ocean sunshine and he basked in the attention of the room. Until one of the crowd said, "Yeah, but we don't get to go fishing today!" A weak-hearted chuckle came from the cabin, most seemed too sick for a joke.

Steven just shrugged off the comment, like he had some inside knowledge. I would bet he did.

Coming back into sight of the jetty was the most welcome sight of my life. I didn't care if I saw a whale jump or not, I wanted back on land. It turned out that almost the whole tuna fleet in Newport had turned around that morning. Only one boat had made it to the happy fishing grounds 50 miles out to sea. That boat, with twelve passengers on board, caught a grand total of six fish. Bad odds.

My group and I had made the migration from the high desert for some seafood, not a seasick boat ride. Credits were issued to the passengers. The guide service, Captains Reel, offered full refunds to those who did not get to go tuna fishing as planned.

Instead of the tuna charter, we settled on a more sedate rockfish trip. They even tossed in some crab pots as an extra bonus for the hassle with tuna fishing.

After an hour on dry land we were underway, dropping crab pots and finding secret fishing holes. I prepared for the second excursion by eating an egg sandwich, taking some Dramamine and insisting on standing, not sitting, the whole boat ride. I felt like a million hung out to dry bucks.

Rock fishing is not exactly a technical affair. You drop the line into the water, wait for it to hit bottom and then slowly jig it back to the surface. Sure, you can develop a style – like letting the jig sit closer to the bottom longer hoping to catch a lingcod. Or you can just slowly retrieve not jigging. You can change colors like you would with bass. It is all your choice. You also run the risk of catching bottom and snagging, a lot.

Each and every time I would feel the tug of a fish at the end of my line I would set the hook like I was trying to lodge a section of wrought iron into the fishes face. Apparently, this is not the way to fish for the soft face rock fish. They have a mouth like a wet cardboard box, despite looking like a very close relative to the largemouth bass with its famous hard mouth. I would get repeated warnings from Steven to not set the hook. "I have, no shit, seen a full set of lips come to the surface with no fish attached." Gives a whole new meaning to "rippin'" lips now don't it.

But being a good steelhead, bass, trout and catfisherman I will always set the hook. Nothing I can do about that, I'm afraid. "Just try and resist the urge, you will catch more fish," Steven said. Setting the hook or not in three and a half hours we had our limit of rock-fish and were on our way back to the jetty. Seven fish for me, twenty-one between the three of us, a nice haul considering our tuna adventure had ended with zero fish.

When we hauled the crab pots on board, a surprisingly difficult task that sent my father chumming the front of the boat, we had twenty-one keeper crabs for the boat. That would mean a little over three crabs per person in our little group. Not exactly the meat run we had been hoping for with the tuna. Most times the tuna boats catch about five fish per person, on average about 15 pounds each.

Rockfish are a different story all together. At the dock I watched in amazement as the fish filleter made short work of our catch. A few quick and simple cuts and our catch was a manageable pile in plastic bags. Five pounds of fish fillets per person.

It was worth every dollar not to have to clean them myself. Boiling and cleaning the crab was also well worth the meager price of cleaning. I fully recommend the service for those who don't live close by. He took a whole mess of fish and turned them into a freezer bag of goodness.

At seventy bucks per person it is hard to find a better deal for entertainment than fishing. Newport offers various fishing charters, museums, jetties, shops and piers and is the perfect place to get seasick…I mean spend the family vacation and sneak in a quick fishing trip.

Grilled Albacore Tuna (or sea bass) if you are desperate

Serves 4

4 6 oz. fillets – the ones from your favorite catch that day
Olive oil
1 clove garlic, chopped
1 tablespoon freshly ground pepper
Salt
1 tablespoon fennel seeds, rough cracked in spice grinder or mortar

Preheat the grill. Season the fillets with pepper, garlic, salt and fennel seeds. Flip and repeat. When your beer is open and you are near the grill pour JUST a little oil onto the fish and rub it in. If you add the oil as the first step the seasoning will fall off.

Grill about 2 minutes per side. Pull the fish off the barbecue and let sit for 5 minutes while reminiscing about how much of a fight she put up while out on the water.

Sweet Corn and Dungeness Crab Sauce

2 ears fresh corn, shucked
1 cup chicken stock
1 clove garlic, crushed and chopped
¼ cup whipping cream
Picked meat from one large crab
Salt and freshly ground pepper
1 tablespoon chopped fresh tarragon
Chive for garnish

Cut the kernels from the corncob. The sharper the knife the better. Carefully scrape the cut side of the cob down onto the cutting board with the backside of the knife. You will see a white viscous liquid come out of the cob (I call this corn juice) and it has a ton of flavor. Reserve the corn and juice in a small bowl. Cut the bare cobs in half lengthwise.

Bring the chicken stock and the corncobs to a simmer in a small pot over medium-high heat. Let simmer for 20 minutes. Remove the cobs and discard. Add the garlic, corn kernels and juice to the simmering chicken stock.

The freshness of the corn, time of year and other factors will affect the amount of time it takes to thicken the sauce – it could be 5 minutes of simmering or it could be 30 seconds. Watch closely and when the sauce has thickened slightly add the cream and season with salt and pepper. Taste and adjust seasonings. Simmer for a few moments and remove from heat.

Immediately before serving, toss the crabmeat and fresh tarragon with the corn sauce. Serve over fish.

30

HOW NOT TO CATCH SURFPERCH

In the back of my mind, I knew that I really should not be fishing right now. The wind was blowing the snow into drifts, then the drifts were being covered with sand and then snow, then sand, then snow creating a mesmerizing layer cake pattern. I punched holes into the drifts with my hip-wader boots. The slowly receding tide was freezing as it rolled out; the breaking ice crunching as I walked. I do not make it to the coast often, so I needed to take advantage of this surfperch fishing opportunity.

Why? Because I have never caught one. Like ever. Seriously, never. Embarrassing, right?

This boney little fish has become my Pacific Ocean nemesis. I wish it was a white whale, or a blue marlin, or even a sail fish in Cabo San Lucas. But no, it's a perch.

I am at a loss as to why I can't seem to land this bluegill of the sea. I watch people catch five-gallon buckets full, tossing out little hunks of clam and sand shrimp that look no different from my bait. Fishing is one of my strong points as an outdoorsman; I know when to set the hook.

I have fished for surfperch during low tide, high tide, slack tide, hot weather, snowstorms and rainstorms. The one saving grace about my perch deficit is that it seems that I can catch everything but surfperch. To date, off the coast of Central Oregon and Northern California, I have caught the following species: bream, grouper, mackerel, rockfish (like 10 types), lingcod, Dungeness crab, red crab, greenling and one ugly SOB I could not identify so I tossed it back.

Almost all of these fish are great eating. The only one that is questionable is mackerel, which is a fishy-fish. Some say that all mackerel is good for is cat food. I disagree; it also makes wonderful bait and exceptional sushi.

Over the years of not catching surfperch I have come up with a three golden rules, if I follow these rules (and I nearly compulsively do) I can almost guarantee myself a deficit of surfperch.

Rule #1- Fish Near the Rocks

Being an inland fisherman, I have a habit of looking for structure when I fish. The idea of just casting off the sand into the surf is hard for me to swallow. Just like my lake fish and river trout, I assume that fish want something to hide behind or near or under.

Surfperch have no fascination with structure. Instead, they live in that little trough that is formed by the waves wearing away the sandy bottom. The water movement in this trough stirs up all sorts of critters and sends them floating into the deep blue sea. The surfperch eat these little floating crabs and clams. The goal for a fisherman is to cast a hunk of meat into the trough and hope that a perch strikes.

If you want to pretend to be perch fishing, then you should fish near a rock outcropping or off jetties. I cast out into the surf, randomly guessing where the trough is, with my fingers crossed the surfperch will bite. Then I slowly retrieve my line towards the rocks. I feel more comfortable this way, even if it is totally wrong. Fishing this way will almost certainly land you something other than perch.

Rule #2 - Don't Poke Pole

It was low tide in the Newport Jetty. In a fit of boredom, I started dropping my bait into deep holes – surprisingly, I caught a bunch of fish. Only later did I find out that this is an honest to goodness fishing technique, well, a less refined version of a technique called "poke-poling." The basics of this fishing method are simple – shove bait into the face of an otherwise unbothered fish. The key to success is constant movement and selecting the right hole, the deeper the better. Switch locations if something doesn't bite within the first few seconds; keep bumping down the jetty or rocks looking for a fish to bite. One morning I caught seven in under an hour. I tossed all but one back, but it was a great way to kill a little time wishing for perch. As far as set up is concerned I use the typical surfperch rig, drop shot with two hooks coming off the main line. I use clam, squid, shrimp or artificial night crawlers. At the Newport Jetty most commonly, you'll catch greenling when you're poke-poling. I hear that along the coast of northern California you catch monkeyfaced eels. Not bad options when the surfperch refuse to bite.

Rule #3 - Don't Judge the Man Fishing a Bobber

Look, bobbers and jigs work. Just not on surfperch. I set up a ½ ounce head on one of those big red bobbers from Kmart, maybe about 4-feet of line between the two. Then I'll cast along the rocks and slowly retrieve. I have nailed the heck out of some rockfish this way before. I have never heard of a surfperch caught in this fashion.

A bobber and a sabiki rig (one of those multiple hook jig contraptions) sent into the surf is a total and complete loss. Never ever do that – you end up with a ball of string and hooks. I have caught a whole bunch of bream with a sabiki and a bobber along the rocks, however.

Cooked Bait with Spicy Mustard Greens

Some days you win big fishing, some days you do not. This recipe is for a day when you are forced to eat what most others call bait. It's not halibut, salmon or lingcod – but this recipe will give you crispy skinned fish with great garlic and mustard flavors.

Serves 4

The Bait

8 small "bream" or other bait fish, cleaned and descaled
¼ cup canola oil
1 cup flour
1 tablespoon ground mustard
1 teaspoon cayenne pepper
1 teaspoon salt
1 teaspoon freshly ground pepper
1 tablespoon garlic powder

Preheat oven to "warm" or lowest setting.

Combine flour and spices in a bowl. Wet the fish slightly and dredge in flour. Wet again and re-dredge. This double batter will stick better than a single layer. Double batter all fish and reserve on a lightly-floured cookie sheet.

Heat oil over medium heat in a medium-sized cast iron skillet until it reaches 350°F. To check the temperature of the oil on the stove simply drop small clumps of batter into the oil filled pan. When the batter bubbles quickly and then floats the oil is close to the correct temperature. If the small scrap of batter browns or burns quickly than the oil is too hot.

Fry the fish for 3-4 minutes on each side, or until the fish turns golden brown and delicious (GB&D). Transfer the cooked fish to a paper-towel-lined cookie sheet in the warm oven.

Spicy Mustard Greens

To compensate for fried food I always like a little sautéed super-food as an accompaniment. Oh, and mustard greens taste great, too.

The spiciness of mustard greens can vary dramatically from field to field and from day to day. Always taste before serving – if the greens are too bitter, add sugar, if they are mild and bland, add Sriracha. Either way, season with salt and pepper.

1 tablespoon butter
1 lb. mustard greens
4 cloves garlic, crushed
1 teaspoon sugar (optional)
1 teaspoon Sriracha (optional)
Salt and freshly ground pepper

Heat butter in a medium sauté pan over medium heat. Add the mustard greens and garlic. Cook 2-3 minutes until wilted and tender.

Serve the greens over the top of the fried fish.

31

EAT THE INVADERS

Text message exchange with Professor Steve Young, College of Western Idaho, Biology Chair
Me – We spoke the other day about eating snails. Is the variety in my hand edible?
Steve – Ah…very nice. Everything is edible Randy! Those are of no conservation interest if that is what you are asking.
Me – So they aren't going to kill me then…great.
Steve – Ha! I doubt it. Cook them though.

It was Father's Day at Duffy Pond in Middleton and I noticed the biggest snail I had ever seen. Now, normally, a snail does not catch my attention. But this one was no ditch bank jobber; it was the size of a half dollar coin. Not only was the snail large, but he had an abundance of buddies around. The shallow water seemed to have a big snail every square foot or so, and I could see them stretching out across the bottom of the pond.

I never would have thought that Idaho could produce a snail that large. Big snails, to me, are tropical creatures. Last I checked freezing was hard on snails.

I immediately started having hunger pangs. I admit it's a sad state of affairs that my initial instinct, when I see something in nature, is to figure out if it is food.

As a classically trained chef, I know escargot are delicious and are considered a delicacy in many parts of the world. France has escargot, India has the cinnamon snail and San Francisco has a garden goodie called the periwinkle. All are eaten and enjoyed, so why the heck can't we eat Idaho pond snails. Right?

But I was hesitant to pluck this mud bug out of the moss-covered water and eat it. A year or so earlier I had stuck my foot in my mouth about wild-gathered foods in a very public way. I claimed you could eat the clams out of the Snake River during an interview with Guy Hand on his public radio show *Edible Idaho*. I was proven wrong by a biologist from the College of Western Idaho named Steve Young. Apparently, mercury and other toxins build up in the long-living Asian clams that I was eating. In no hurry to repeat my self-poisoning, I decided to contact Steve again about the snails.

As it happens, Steve is the author of a convenient little book called *A Guide to Southern Idaho's Freshwater Mollusks.* I mean, really, could it have been any easier? (Had I bothered to read this book I would not have been eating the Snake River clams…)

According to the book these types of snails, *Radix auricularia*, are not commonly found in the Treasure Valley. They are most often located in the Wood River Valley, near Sun Valley, and in the Bruneau River area. Originally imported from Europe to control algae blooms, they are also called "Big Ear" snails because of the large aperture that makes a distinctive ear shape on their shells.

When I got the all clear from the Professor, I went back out to Duffy Pond. I was armed with a pair of hip waders, a small mesh bag and a leaf rake. It did not take long before I had about three dozen snails.

I put the snails on ice and drove them back to my house. The typical method for preparing wild caught snails is to let them "clean" themselves in cornmeal in a wooden box. You replace the water and cornmeal every other day for about a week, which gives the snails long enough to discharge whatever they had been eating and stuff themselves to the gills with cornmeal. I love this method, because I don't particularly like the taste of half-digested pond algae in my food.

After the snails have had time to clean themselves out, the next step is to blanch them in boiling salt water. After cooking them for about five minutes, you "shock" them in ice water. Then the tricky part: getting them out of the shell.

The shape of the snail shell makes it difficult to remove the meat – I use a chopstick or even a small skewer to gently swirl the meat out of the shell.

Apparently, I must have struck at the exact wrong time of the year for harvesting the snails because every other snail was full of tiny snails, shells and all. I didn't feel too bad about killing the breeding adults since the snails are invasive. But my gut did churn a little when cutting the baby shells out of the meat

With the meat removed, I then froze them for good measure. Many methods can be used to kill stray bacteria; I like the combination of boiling and freezing.

My snail preparation was simple and classic: I cut the snails in ¼ inch chunks and boiled the bejesus out of them in sherry and garlic. I added a little roasted red pepper for good measure and baked them with breadcrumbs and Parmesan. I tested my wild snail concoction out on the staff of *The Boise Weekly*. In a swanky downtown bar, I rolled in with a soup bowl full of cooked snail and passed it around with little crostini toasts. It was well-received, though most eaters had a look of shock on their face when I explained the dish.

While searching for snails, I watched a pair of common turtles swim off a log and into the murky water. I recognized them as distinctly different from the native painted turtle from up north. These guys were house pets that now have a breeding population. So it seems that I must figure out how to catch a turtle. I am saving the environment, after all. Turtle soup anyone? Anyone?

32

FROGGER

Blame it on *Duck Dynasty*, or maybe on the cacophonous croaking of frogs along the canal near my house, but I have developed an itch for bullfrog gigging.

Frog gigging is considered a summertime pleasure to many of my Southern-born friends. It is a right of passage to muck through the swamp after amphibians. Gigging frogs is a time-honored tradition for gathering grub – though not necessarily in Idaho. Warmer climates and abundant swampy areas tend to encourage frog populations, while our high desert state is not known for its swamps. But I love to eat me some frog legs, and I really wanted to start a frog-hunting tradition for my family.

Proper gigging requires special equipment. Most notable is the gig spear tip: envision Neptune's trident but frog-sized. None of my local sporting goods stores carry frog-gigging equipment, so I found a four-tined spear tip for $3 online and ordered two. When they arrived in the mail a few days later, I headed to the lawn and garden department of Walmart and purchased a bamboo stick. I attached the spear tip to the stick and was on my way to find a gigging spot.

First, I had to find out where the city would allow me to do it. No one was quite sure what to make of the guy calling the City of Boise to ask if he could gig frogs in city limits; my inquiry was met with an awkward silence on the other end of the phone line. Fishing is allowed in city limits at the river and various ponds throughout Boise, but the idea of a guy with a gig spear wandering around Ann Morrison Park seemed to have people on edge. So I abandoned Boise and called the City of Nampa. No awkward silences there. I got a quick and easy "go for it." As long as I did not throw the spear and was not in a city park after dark, Nampa said that I could gig to my heart's content.

Grandpa, two of my boys and I made the "just past bedtime" trek to a local pond. A frog hunter listens for the telltale croak, a low guttural sound reminiscent of a bull cow. We could hear the croaking of frogs from hundreds of yards away. I stepped into the pond and my boots sank about a foot into water that smelled like rotten eggs. Our hunting posse split into two teams, each going a different direction around the pond. I carried my younger son through the muck. We saw frogs immediately.

The normal pattern for frog hunting, developed over thousands of years, is for the frog hunter to creep slowly and silently toward the beasts, while lowering his spear in the direction of the frog. Just prior to the frog escaping in a dramatic leap, the hunter must stab the frog. At the last moment most frogs dart into the water, escaping the hunter. Sure, some don't make it quickly enough, but this stalk-and-dart routine is a well-established pattern. Some frogs float out in the water making for harder targets. Other frogs kindly wait on the banks. Some croak loudly and bound across the top of the water to freedom.

The flashlight gives the modern hunter a notable advantage. Frogs cannot resist the power of our Duracells. The frogger shines a light across a body of water until the light reflects back from a frog's eyes. At that point, the hunter must keep the light on the frog to keep it mesmerized, a small movement of the light allows the frog to break the trance and duck

away. A quick spear thrust into the frog and then a quick scooping motion bringing the tip of the gig toward the sky should seal the deal. If all goes well, the hunter has just bagged part of a nice meal.

At one point on our excursion, we could see at least twenty-seven sets of eyes gleaming back at us, entranced. Game time. The bullfrogs darted, dived, croaked and though we missed more shots than we landed the sheer numbers of available frogs allowed for ample picking. Sixteen frogs later (four for each of us), we walked back to the truck. Our heaviest frog was just less than two pounds; he was a total toad.

We took them back to the house and transformed them from Nampa pond-jumpers to gourmet frog legs, French-style.

Frogs have a curious culinary history with a connection to the Catholic Church. Having been classified as fish rather than meat and with a number of meatless days per year dictated by the church, dutiful Catholics in France made the frog leg a national food treasure for the country, if not the world. In the United States, frog legs show up in traditional Cajun and Creole cooking, both of which, of course, have roots in French cuisine. The tradition of eating frogs hasn't really ever hit it big in Idaho. In fact, I usually get a turned-up nose when I tell people about frog gigging. But that is not a deterrent for me.

We soaked the legs overnight in milk to help purge the vague sulfur smell of the pond. Then we battered and fried them outside on the barbecue.

It was a culinary revelation: I have had frog legs from San Francisco to Macau, but I've never eaten them fried. They were addictive. The meat was as white as cream and as soft as a poached baby chicken. Not a hint of pond. Three generations of King boys chowed down on the frogs and made plans for further excursions.

Fried Frog Legs

Don't mess with perfection. Those Southern boys and girls who love them some good ol' fashioned fried frog legs are on to something – they are delicious. This recipe comes courtesy of my East Texas buddy John – it's how his momma makes frog legs. Cooking them is easy: "get a Dutch oven and fill it with about two or three inches of fry oil. You know Crisco or canola, whatever," according to John. "Then you deep fry them until they are brown."

Serves 4

Cut the frogs in half then pretend you are taking the pants off them with a pair of pliers, no joke. Brine the meat in salt water for 24 hours. This will do two things. One, it will make most of the big black veins turn translucent and thus more palatable. Two, the salt water will keep the meat moist during the cooking process.

12 pairs of frog legs
1 cup flour
1 teaspoon cayenne pepper
1 tablespoon salt
1 tablespoon freshly ground pepper
3 cups Crisco or canola oil
1 cup milk

Preheat oil in a Dutch oven to 350°F.

Mix dry ingredients in a small bowl and place the milk in another small bowl.

Remove the frogs from the brine and pat dry with a paper towel. Roll them in flour mixture, then dunk them in milk. This will create a sticky surface for the second dredging of flour. Next roll and lightly press the flour on the frog legs.

Fry the legs until golden brown, approximately 4-5 minutes. Transfer to a plate lined with paper towels. Sprinkle with lemon juice, if desired.

33

CITY FISHING

I used to laugh at the guys I saw fishing the little culverts and canals in my hometown. They seemed unshaven, scraggly, and maybe even in a bad mood when I drove by in my ratty old car. I could not understand why they would waste their time fishing the canals when all that they held were sucker fish and some trout. It seemed illogical. After all, good fishing was only about an hour away.

Twenty years later and I find myself on Saturday mornings – bleary-eyed, unshaven and wearing a grease-stained Carhartt, fishing a culvert within the city limits of Nampa. I am the guy the teenagers yell at when they drive by in their ratty old cars.

But I get it now. I no longer fear being seen by the side of the road fishing. No social anxiety stresses me out. I have moved beyond embarrassment in life. I have three children, after all. I get why they would take a few hours before the rest of the family wakes up and toss a line in a canal. The goal is not to land a trophy but to be *out*. Out of the house. Out of the stress. I have concluded that it is a good thing to take a break from the worries and engagements that cause so much anxiety in day-to-day life. Even if you are home before *SpongeBob* comes on TV.

When I am canal fishing my expectations are low. I know that I will not land a lunker bass, a trophy brown trout or a bucket head catfish (all of which are available within one hour drive time from my house). But with low expectations comes low gear requirements.

I normally bait fish when canal fishing. Casting a lure in a canal just seems wrong to me – it makes me feel like I am trying too hard. Lord knows that I don't bust out the St. Croix fly pole either. Oh, man that would be pretentious.

My bait comes from one of two places. The first place is from below my foam archery target. It normally holds a few night crawlers and some trout specials – if I am desperate I will peel back the plastic around the flowerbeds for some worms. The second place that I check is the bottom of my fishing bag, normally there are a few chunks of semi-dry Powerbait that can be salvaged. Worms and Powerbait go into the same small Tupperware container and slide into my jacket pocket. Toss in a few hooks, a package of swivels and a pack of egg weights and I am ready to head out the door. No big tackle necessary.

Although I have low expectations, I do not stick to the same locations week to week. I virtually scout my prospective fishing holes via Google Earth. I take a canal that I have either seen people fishing in or have thought would hold fish and trace it back to the source. Most time this is a larger canal or a small river. Most times these are great spots to fish. The water being spilled over from one body to another creates a small "hole" that holds fish.

I will stand on the top of the pipe or whatever the water is coming out from and simply drop my line and count to six. Then I flip the reel and let the water take the bait to the left side of the hole. I give it a few minutes and then retrieve. I drop my bait and count to five before flipping my reel and waiting. Then four. I repeat until both sides of the "hole" have been fished.

Most times I catch a carp, a whitefish or a sucker but seldom do I go home having been skunked. On the off chance I do catch a trout, I keep it and eat it. While they do not have the same flavor as a high mountain stream trout, they are considerably cheaper (you get what you pay for!).

Canal fishing, often near your own house, is seldom glorious. A person should not go looking to score points on Facebook with friends or text buddies the pics. It is simply for the *joy of going fishing.*

Smoked Trout Chowder

I usually smoke canal trout. Why? As my buddy Ryan puts it they can taste like "the swamp you caught them in…" True enough. Throughout the winter and the spring I catch small trout and freeze them. Eventually I have enough that I smoke a batch and make some chowder.

This is a quick and easy "Manhattan-style" chowder. I do the scare quotes on "Manhattan" because I am not from the Northeast and my mother did not teach me some old family recipe for this. Plus, this dish has a Latin kick with jalapeño peppers and lime juice.

Serves 2

1 10-12 inch smoked trout, picked and boneless
1 tablespoon butter
2 slices of bacon, sliced into strips
2 red potatoes, diced
1 jalapeño, halved
½ white onion, diced
2 tomatoes, diced
1 stalk celery, diced
1 carrot, diced
1 lime, quartered
1 cup tomato juice
Salt and freshly ground pepper
Fresh mint
Sour cream

Melt butter in a medium-sized sauce pan over medium heat. Add bacon and cook until crispy, about 4 minutes. Add the red potatoes, jalapeño, onion, tomatoes, celery, and carrot. Sauté until the onions are translucent, about 5-6 minutes. Squeeze the lime into the mixture and deglaze the bottom of the pan. Add the tomato juice to the pan. The juice should be enough to just barely cover the vegetables.

Season with salt and pepper and bring to a simmer. When the potato is tender gently fold in the smoked trout.

Garnish with sour cream and mint.

Wild Onion and Mustard Trout

This recipe came from sheer necessity. I was a college student returning home to Boise from Moscow and I had just enough money for gas. But, I was hungry. The gas station attendant was nice enough to let me have some mustard packets so I stopped on the Little Salmon River, pulled out my fly rod from behind the seat, caught three fish and cooked 'em up. The pan fries held me over until I arrived in Boise and could eat cold pizza from my parent's fridge. I've served slightly more sophisticated versions in restaurants since, but this simple method still has a sentimental spot in my heart.

3 freshly-caught trout
2 packets yellow mustard
Wild onions, a handful

Catch fish, gut fish, stuff fish with wild onions, wrap fish in foil, toss fish in the fire, cook fish, take fish out of the fire, remove foil, peel back skin, slather in mustard, eat.

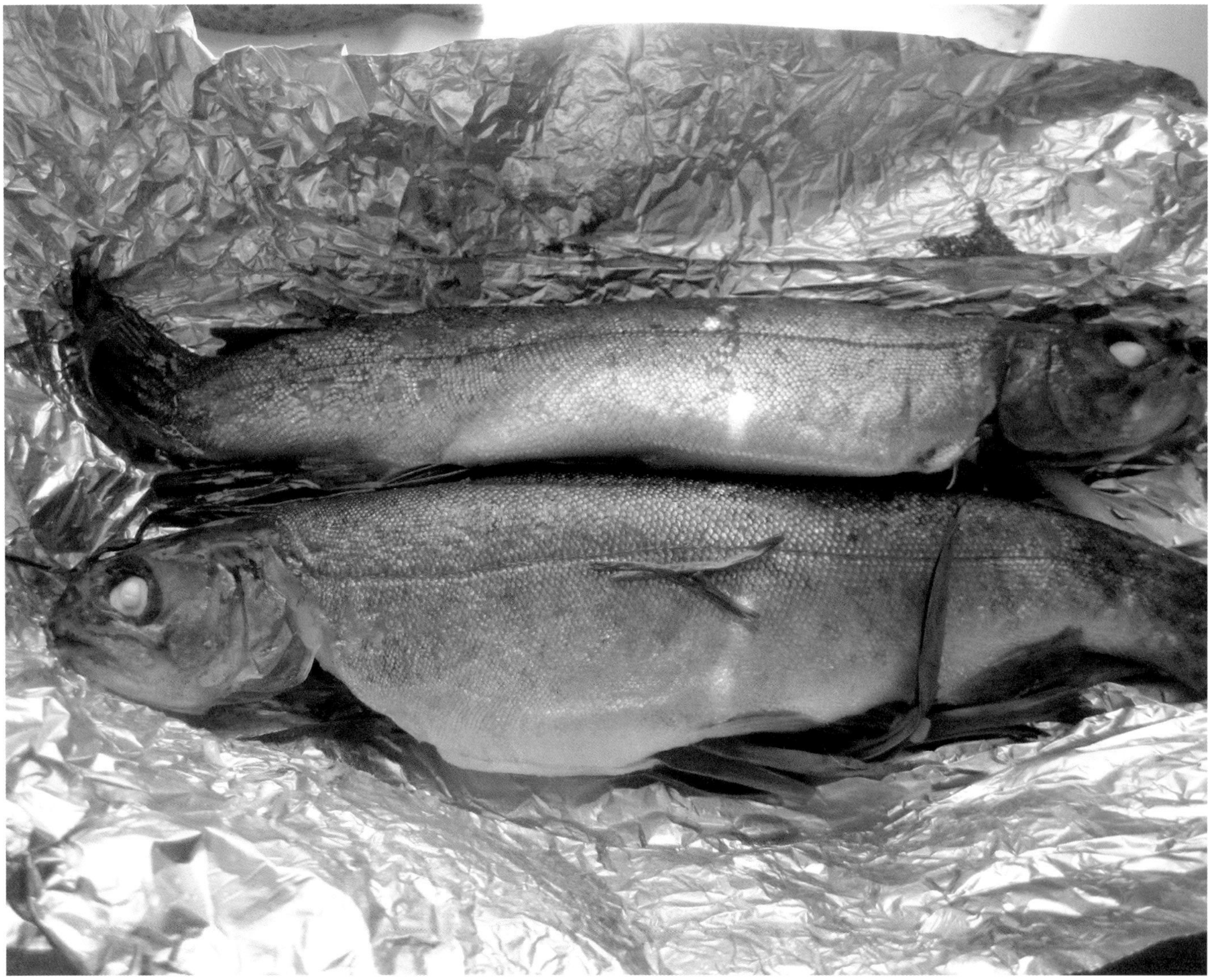

HOME

We left the beach for the hills,
scouring the duff for mushrooms
before hitting the mother lode,
about ten pounds of fall porcini –
giant mushrooms
with unforgettable flavor.

34

FORAGING

The world has changed – my world has changed. Most of my life has been spent outdoors with a gun, bow or fishing pole in my hand. I can remember being allowed to go pheasant hunting, alone, before I was 10.

I always knew there was another side to the hunter-gatherer equation, but I had never taken the time to learn how to properly forage. Sure I picked blackberries and I definitely scoured burns for morels in the spring. But actually foraging, taking the time to view the plants under my feet, has never been on the top of my list.

I have found a mentor in Hank Shaw. His first book *Hunt, Gather, Cook* is a primer for all things wild. From his book I learned about sea peas, and the ornamental plums that are in my suburban neighborhood. Hank keeps a James Beard Award winning website as well: honest-food.net, where I frequently gather information on gathering and cooking projects.

Recently I have had the pleasure of getting to forage with Hank. At an inconspicuous beach in Northern California, Hank immediately pointed out wild edibles: curly dock, sorrel, cow parsnip, California bay, New Zealand spinach. Sure, I had seen many of them before but I did not know their names and would have never eaten them.

As Hank showed me each plant, I would pick a section and taste it. Some tasted delicious; others made me want to gag. This prompted Hank to say, "Foraging with chefs is like foraging with babies, all you do is stick things in your mouth." Valuable lesson: just because things are edible, they do not always taste good in their raw state.

We left the beach for the hills, scouring the duff for mushrooms before hitting the mother lode, about ten pounds of fall porcini – giant mushrooms with unforgettable flavor. Hank was gleeful, though I struggled to share the same level of enthusiasm. Mushrooms? It was only later that I realized just how special the find was: it was like catching a steelhead on the first cast, something that never happens.

On my return to Idaho, I saw the sprouting green things around me differently. I spotted wild mint growing on the hill next to work. I gathered curly dock and dandelions from a park along the Boise River. I picked a patch of nettles by the canal near my house and found salsify on the ignored side of my backyard fence. There was lambs quarter in the rose beds and beggar's purse in the garden.

Later that spring I furthered my gathering skills with Darcy Williamson of Mavens Haven in McCall. We teamed up for a foraging and cooking weekend. With Darcy I learned a ton about foraged food in my native Idaho. Plants that I have ignored for years – the flowers with edible bulbs, the wild garlic, the miners lettuce, the fiddlehead ferns and many others.

Darcy and I hiked the woods near Riggins. It was an odd feeling to have my head down looking for wild plants and mushrooms instead of up looking for wild game. Each mushroom gave me a temporary moment of happiness, not as large a bump as an elk or a deer would have but still a very real boost. Every thing I dug up was a present from Mother Earth.

As amazing as foraging was I couldn't help but look for game – turkey season, though I had left my gun at home on purpose so I wouldn't be distracted from my foraging. Of course, anytime I leave my gun behind game presents itself – we saw a gobbler not 30 feet off the road. We could have had turkey for dinner but instead found dinner growing out of the side of a spring, under a fallen pine and buried deep below a flowering bulb. I knew what I had foraged tasted just as good as any wild turkey.

35

SIDE DISHES AND SALADS

Butter and Morels

When I get back from morel hunting the first thing that I do is eat a plate full. I don't mess around with fancy preparations because they are perfect as is: they smell of the forest, bite like meat and are highly nutritious. Note: morels contain toxins and should never be eaten raw.

Serves 1 greedy person

12 oz. morels, halved and washed
¼ cup butter
Fistful of wild onions or 2 green onions, sliced thin
Salt and freshly ground pepper

Melt butter in a medium-sized skillet. Add the mushrooms and season with salt and pepper. Cook morels until they just start to seep liquid back into the pan. Remove pan from heat and let rest for 2 minutes. Sprinkle with onions and eat them right out of the pan.

Hattie's Mashers

It is a proud and sad moment in my life when my wife can cook something better than me. After all, I am the professional. Right?

Serves 5

3½ lbs. Idaho russet potatoes
1¼ cups milk
1 cup butter, 2 sticks, cut into cubes
2 cloves garlic, crushed then minced
1 tablespoon salt
Freshly ground pepper

Peel and dice potatoes – cut them all about the same size, roughly ½ inch square. Place potatoes in a large saucepan filled with water and ½ tablespoon of salt. Bring to a boil, turn heat down and simmer for about 20 minutes. The potatoes should offer no resistance when poked with a fork; the water should be slightly cloudy with potato bits.

Drain and return to pot. Heat potatoes, milk, butter and garlic over medium-low. Mash with either a potato masher or, preferably, a wire whisk. When I say mash I mean mash the bejesus out of them. Mash for a solid 4-5 minutes until every conceivable chunk of potato is transformed into a fluffy white creaminess. Think about a teenager that is frustrating you, mix a little longer. Season with salt and pepper then mash them a little more to incorporate. Taste, adjust salt and pepper level.

Let stand, covered, for 5-10 minutes so that the potatoes have time to readjust to life after being mashed. This will greatly improve their texture, thickness and attitude.

Pico de Gratin

While it might not be an original idea to combine potatoes and salsa this application and method is certainly not the norm. These potatoes go well with just about everything – breakfast, lunch or dinner. We make them a lot in Dutch ovens and this is a forgiving recipe to practice your briquette skills on. I am not a Dutch oven master but I can pull these potatoes off with little trouble.

Serves 5

3 lbs. red potatoes
1 cup salsa
1 cup water
½ cup all-purpose flour
12 oz. cheddar, jack or other flavorful cheese, grated
Salt and freshly ground pepper

Heat your briquettes. You will need 25 or so for this recipe. A 400°F oven will work, too.

Slice potatoes thinly to form little potato coins, about ¼-inch thick. Mix the salsa, water and flour in a small bowl. In a medium-sized Dutch arrange the potatoes in concentric rings, seasoning each layer with a little salt and pepper. Pour the salsa mix over the top of the potatoes. Top with cheese.

Cook for 1 hour with ten coals on the bottom and 15 on the top, or for about 1 hour and 15 minutes in a 400°F oven. The cheese should be golden brown and the potatoes soft. Remove from heat and let stand for about 15 minutes, this will give the potatoes time to absorb left over moisture and make them easier to cut.

Coconut Rice

White rice is a weakness for me. I know I am supposed to eat wild, brown, red, black and all the colors that are not white. But, alas, I have a special place in my heart for good ol' white. This recipe, and versions of it, are common all over the country and hail from Hawaiian cooking. I think the mantra over there is "sweet is good and sweeter is better." My inspiration for this is a good chef buddy and friend Mike Mohica. His rice is just grubbin'.

Vital to all preparations of white rice is the starch rinse. I find the pot I am going to cook the rice in and pour in my rice. Then I fill the pot to the top with water and give it a good hand toss. This will get most of the starch off the rice. Then I pour the water off and fill it up again tossing the rice in the water. You will notice that the water turns white when you rinse the rice in it. This is the starch that makes rice "gummy" when you cook it. If you rinse your rice you are more likely to get that light fluffy rice that you love, not a clumpy mess. Strain the rice by pouring it into a colander. It is now ready to use.

Serves 4

1 12 oz. can sweetened coconut milk
¼ cup water
1 cup Calrose or jasmine rice
Salt and freshly ground pepper

Bring ingedients to a boil in a medium-sized pot. Cover and turn off the heat. The residual heat will cook the rice in about 12-15 minutes. Don't take the lid off or the heat will dissipate and you can get "crunchy" rice, nobody likes crunchy rice.

As important to this dish as the rice cooking is the rice garnishing. I like to use that ridiculously sweet baking coconut for this application, by the way.

Garnish

¼ cup coconut flake
1 tablespoon black sesame seeds

Add the coconut to a small sauté pan and place in the oven. Turn on the oven to "broil" and cook until it is brown, not black on the top. Cool and sprinkle over the rice with the sesame seeds. The combination is visually striking and very grubbin'.

Mac n' Cheese with Duck Confit and Whisky

Most years I have a jar of confit meat sitting in my fridge. It is covered in fat and will last for months – sometimes its duck, sometimes its rabbit – heck one time it was raccoon. I follow the recipe on page 72 and the results are delicious. What I do with this meat varies. A favorite is confit mac n' cheese. Gourmet mac n' cheese is worth the effort, especially with the addition of a little whisky.

Serves 6

½ pound cavatappi (elbow macaroni will work, too)
4 tablespoons butter, divided
1 small onion, diced
1 cup confit meat
¼ cup whisky – something you would drink, not swill
1 egg
½ cup evaporated milk
¼ cup milk
1 teaspoon Sriracha
Salt and freshly ground pepper
¼ teaspoon fresh nutmeg
10 oz. cheddar, grated

Bring a large pot of salted water to a boil. Cook pasta until al dente (soft but with a little crunch left) and drain. Toss pasta with 2 tablespoons of butter to coat – this will keep the pasta from sticking together.

Melt the remaining butter over medium heat in the now empty pot. Just before it browns add the diced onion and the confit. Cook for 2 minutes. Add the whisky and simmer until reduced by half, about 2 more minutes.

Blend egg, condensed milk, milk, nutmeg and Sriracha in a small bowl. Add to confit mixture slowly while stirring constantly. Add pasta, mix well. Slowly stir in the cheese. Mix until all the cheese is incorporated and the sauce is creamy and thick. Serve hot.

Jalapeño Cornbread

The extent to which I love the combination of sweet and spicy knows no bounds. I consider myself an addict of that flavor combination. This recipe is a prime example, sweet corn and honey combined with the flash of heat from a jalapeño.

Serves 4

1⅔ cups cornmeal
2 to 3 cups all-purpose flour
½ cup sugar
2 teaspoons baking soda
1¼ cups milk
4 teaspoons butter
2 eggs
1 cup plain yogurt
4 jalapeños, diced
1 cup honey

Preheat oven to 350°F.

Bring milk almost to a boil, also known as scalding the milk. When milk is hot melt in the butter. Cool to room temperature. Add yogurt and eggs, stir until well combined.

Sift the dry ingredients in a separate bowl. Add the milk mixture and blend to a smooth batter. Pour into 8 in. x 8 in. baking dish. Top with jalapeños and drizzle honey over the top.

Bake 40-45 minutes.

Dandelion Salad

My wife calls me a "weed eater" when I show up with a bowl of dandelion greens from my yet to be planted garden. The weed seems to grow everywhere so I eat it. What surprises most people is the nutritional value of a dandelion. To paraphrase the author Hank Shaw, wild spring greens make spinach look like a Twinkie. I mix my dandelion greens with the arugula that never seems to die by the back door for a great salad.

Serves 1

1 hard-boiled egg, preferably a duck egg
1 tablespoon Balsamic vinegar
1 tablespoon olive oil
1 teaspoon honey
1 teaspoon stone-ground mustard
Dash Worcestershire sauce
Freshly ground pepper
2 cups wild-gathered greens
2 tablespoons toasted pumpkin seeds (pepitas)

Whisk together the vinegar, oil, honey, Worchestershire and mustard in a medium-sized bowl. Crush the egg with a fork into the dressing until only BB-sized chunks remain. Toss in the greens. Sprinkle with pumpkin seeds.

Asparagus and Wild Mint Salad

Just about the best damn thing on the planet is a plate of wild asparagus. I have a few spots that I go to every year and I guard them with my life. My father doesn't even know where they are. I gather as many as I can each time and then break the stalks on the ones that have started branching. My grandmother told me to do this so the plant would keep sending up new, tender and tasty shoots.

Serves 2-3

10-12 medium-sized asparagus stalks, sliced at an angle into ½-inch lengths
½ lemon, zested and juiced
10 fresh mint leaves, thinly sliced
Extra virgin olive oil
Salt and freshly ground pepper

Fill a medium sized bowl with half ice and half water. Set aside. Bring 2 quarts of water to a boil.

Drop the asparagus into the boiling water. Count to 30 and then remove with a slotted spoon to the ice bath until cool. Remove from the bath and pat dry.

Toss the asparagus with the lemon juice and zest. Sprinkle with mint and a squirt of olive oil. Salt and pepper to taste.

Arugula Salad with Duck Fat and Mulberry Dressing

This dressing goes well with spicy arugula and leftover game meat: I will use confit, velveted goose or turkey ham if I have them. Serve it without meat for a great start to a meal.

Serves 2 entrée, 4 side salad

1 small carrot, shredded
1 small red onion, sliced thin
2 cups arugula
1 cup croutons
¼ cup shaved Parmesan cheese
1 cup cooked wild game meat

Dressing

Necessity is the mother of invention. I was doing some film work for a production company, a demo, and needed to make a "dish in the wild." I was thinking of all the ways that I could connect the salad, and, especially the dressing to the land I was on. I thought back to the winter and about all the ducks I had shot over the area I was going to be filming at. Duck fat, from my confit jar, was on the menu.

Mulberries happened to be ripe at the same time as well. Check, fruit and fat. Next I needed acid. All I could think of was some local vinegar made from Idaho wine. Fruit, fat, acid – the basics of a dressing. I added some salt and it was grubbin'.

¼ cup duck fat
¼ cup olive oil
1 clove garlic, crushed and minced
½ cup ripe mulberries
⅛ cup red wine vinegar
Salt and freshly ground pepper

Pulse the the mulberries, red wine vinegar and garlic in a food processor. While the processor is running, add the duck fat and olive oil. Season to taste with salt and pepper. You might need to add a little sugar, depending on how ripe the mulberries are.

Toss ⅓ cup dressing with vegetables and meat. The greens will naturally rise to the top of the bowl, the croutons and meat will fall to the bottom. This is okay. Place the greens on a plate first then divide the remaining ingredients evenly onto serving plates.

36

SAUCES AND SEASONINGS

Jalapeño, Apricot and Current Jelly

While this is not exactly the jelly Grandma used to make the general idea is still there. I always loved getting jars of this from my paternal grandmother, but it was less the jalapeños and the cider vinegar. Her jelly was more traditional "serve me on toast" kind of concoction. Mine, well mine is for grilling and using as a finishing sauce on smoked meats. Apricots and high desert currents tend to be ripe at about the same time in early summer, so it makes sense that they be served together.

2 jalapeños, diced
2 cups fresh apricots, pits removed
2 cups fresh desert currants
1 cup sugar
1 cup apple cider vinegar
3 oz. pectin
1 white onion, finely diced
2 oz. butter

Heat the butter in a medium sauce pan until melted. Add the onion and cook until translucent. Add the apricots, currants, jalapeños, cider vinegar and sugar. Cook on medium heat for about 25 minutes or until the apricots have broken down into a pulp. Cool slightly and puree in a food processor. Add the pectin and pulse a few times to incorporate. Pour into canning jars. Cool them in a ice-water bath and then freeze them for up to a year. You can also "can" this jelly like my grandmother used to but I am not a pro at this; consult a canning guide book.

Preserved Lemons

The preserved lemon is an oft overlooked and easy to prepare condiment. I love them with grilled fish and meat. They are super easy to prepare in pint-sized mason jars. They keep well for over a year in the fridge.

4 lemons
5 tablespoons salt
2 bay leaves
2 cinnamon sticks
4 whole cloves
White vinegar

Bring a large pot of water to a simmer. Sanitize 2 pint-sized mason jars in water. Place on paper towel to dry. Sanitize lids and rings as well.

Cut the lemons in half and then cut each half into three sections. Toss each lemon in 1 tablespoon of salt. Place two lemons, one bay leaf, one cinnamon stick and two cloves per jar. Pack the lemons in the jar, cover with white vinegar until no lemon is exposed.

Clean the rims of each jar, place canning lids on top, then place rims on. Tighten until "finger" tight. Then place both jars into the boiling water. Simmer for 10 minutes. Remove from the water and let chill on the counter. Listen for the "ping" sound of the jars sealing. Store for one month before using.

Smoked Tomato Sauce

When I get asked how to smoke a tomato my normal response is "carefully and don't inhale." But seriously, a smoked tomato has a lot more layers of flavor than a normal one. Let me rephrase that: a smoked store-bought tomato is a lot better than a not smoked store-bought tomato. A fresh, just-off-the-vine tomato does not need to be smoked and should be used as is.

This recipe is a great way to use those tomatoes that are left on the vine at the end of the year. They might not be totally ripe but you don't want to toss them either. Smoking tomatoes is super easy. Just cut them in half, toss them in oil, salt and pepper and then smoke them for a half an hour. Let cool and remove from the racks. They are now ready for this recipe.

20 smoked tomatoes
¼ cup olive oil
1 cup fresh basil
¼ cup roasted garlic
½ cup tomato paste
Salt and freshly ground pepper to taste

Heat ingredients in a medium sauce pan until hot. Transfer to a food processor and puree until smooth. Cool and reserve. This stuff is great with polenta, fried fish and dark red meats like elk, moose and deer.

Roasted Garlic Puree

It's hard not to like garlic. It is harder not to like roasted garlic. The mild garlic flavor and the applicability in just about any dish make this a food group in many of my kitchens of the past.

Garlic cloves, however much you want to make
Olive oil, enough to cover the garlic

Place the garlic in a small sauce pan and pour in just enough oil to cover. Put a lid on the pan cook over low until the garlic is soft and has turned a nice caramel color, about 20 minutes. This will make your house smell like garlic for a few days, it is worth it.

Pour the leftover garlic into a glass jar with a lid and then let cool to room temperature. Make sure you have enough oil to cover all the garlic cloves in the jar. As long as the garlic is covered it will last in the fridge up to 6 months.

Chipotle Dipping Sauce

2 chipotle peppers (or more, up to 4)
¼ cup lime juice, about 3 limes
3 tablespoons chopped cilantro
1 tablespoon cumin
1 tablespoon roasted garlic puree
2 tablespoons tomato paste
4 egg yolks
1 cup olive oil

Combine all ingredients, except the oil, in a food processor. Pulse a few times to blend. Slowly drizzle the oil in with the processor set to low. This should create an "emulsification" or a thicker mayonnaise-like sauce. Season with salt.

Maple Glaze

Oh, good maple syrup, how I love you. But I also love your cheap counterparts, probably almost as much. This is a sin for a chef, we are held to a standard that more expensive should be better. But for me, the corn syrup with maple flavor is just as good for most cooking applications. Take this recipe. If I used "good" quality syrup it would be wasted on the flavor combination and be overpowering. So, take note you value shoppers…cheap maple syrup has its uses!

⅛ cup honey
1¾ cup maple syrup
3½ oz. chili garlic paste
Juice of 3 limes
1-inch piece ginger

Combine all ingredients in small sauce pot and bring to simmer. Remove from heat, cool and strain. Serve over fish, boar or white-breasted game birds. Great around the holidays for a maple twist with heat.

Camp Meat Rub (Moroccan Spice)

This stuff works on just about everything. I used it the other day on salmon, wild boar tenderloin and venison steaks all at the same time. It is sweet and a little spicy.

¼ cup brown sugar
1 tablespoon paprika
1 tablespoon cumin
1 tablespoon yellow curry powder
1 tablespoon kosher salt
1 teaspoon cinnamon
1 teaspoon dried ginger
½ teaspoon cayenne pepper

Mix all together and let meld for a while. Rub on meat before grilling, roasting, or sautéing. Careful, this mix is high in sugar and can burn quickly. The flavor is well worth it!

Turkey Ham

Making ham gives you delicious meat. I slice it thin for sandwiches, thicker for breakfast or cube it for soup. It gives me more options than traditional roasting. To make turkey ham, you can use a wet or dry cure. This recipe is a wet cure, which uses a salt brine.

Salt is a wonderful preservative. There are many different types of salt. Some are specifically used for curing meat. I use Insta Cure No. 1 for almost everything.

2 quarts hot water
½ cup salt
½ cup white sugar
½ cup brown sugar (or honey)
1 tablespoon Insta Cure No. 1
¼ cup "aromatics"
2 turkey breasts (from one whole bird)

Place the water in a container large enough to hold the liquid and the meal. Stir in the salt, sugar, brown sugar and Insta Cure. Make sure the solids mix well into the liquid. Add the aromatics of your choice, such as orange zest, juniper berries or pickling spices. Use whatever you want to impart additional flavor into the ham. Let the liquid cool a bit.

Add the turkey meat to the cooled liquid. Make sure that all the meat is submerged. Let it brine for a week in the refrigerator.

Remove the turkey from the brine. Pat the meat dry, and let it rest on the counter until it reaches room temperature. Then, smoke the turkey for 4 hours or until it reaches 155°F. If you're not a smoked ham fan simply bake it at 375°F until 155°F at the thickest section. This is very important, the ham will "carry over" to 165°F, necessary for a "kill step" with bacteria. When done, let the ham rest for 30 minutes. This will help retain the moisture.

The ham will last over a week in the fridge and up to a year in the freezer.

Smoked Turkey Gravy

The gobbler has been shot and smoked. You have a wonderful family meal and then are stuck looking at all this meat stuck to the bone. Well, I have a solution. I make a smoked turkey gravy for my breakfast. Smoked turkey has a rich flavor without all the fat that traditional pork sausage contains. Sometimes I even smoke turkeys just to make the gravy…

1 pound smoked turkey (dark meat, white meat, whatever)
½ cup all-purpose flour
3 cups milk
½ stick butter
1 small yellow onion, diced fine
Salt and freshly ground pepper
Fresh herbs – sage, oregano, parsley (no mint, but cilantro is good)

Melt the butter in a medium-sized sauce pot. Add the onion and cook until it turns translucent. Incorporate the turkey with the onion and then sprinkle with flour and stir. When the mixture is lump free add the milk, slowly. Season with salt and pepper. Turn heat down and simmer for about 20 minutes or until it starts to thicken a little bit. Remove from heat and stir in the finishing herbs. Serve over your favorite biscuit recipe.

37

BEVERAGES

Elderberry Bourbon

Elderberries are a diabolical little berry. The berries are insanely bitter while green, they have poisonous stems, poisonous leaves and are totally abundant; fussing and fighting to be eaten and not to be eaten. I like to take mine and do two things – juice them for jelly and to infuse my booze with them.

When infusing booze I ride a fine line. Good booze should be enjoyed as it is, while crappy booze can't be covered up. I like the middle of the road stuff for infusing. I like my sweets as well, so when I gather the elderberries I often let them freeze on the vine. Two brothers I know will watch the weather reports in the fall like hawks and wait for the freeze to go and fill up the back of a truck with elderberries. They use machetes, no shit. Like with ice-wine grapes, sugars become more abundant after the freeze, and tapping into that sugar can greatly improve an elderberry taste.

1 cup frozen elderberries
1 pint Kentucky Bourbon
A glass jar

Put the elderberries in the jar mashing them a little with a fork. Add the pint of Bourbon. Cover tightly and let sit in the fridge for a month. Sip on the booze and sprinkle the berries over ice cream.

Huckleberry Vodka

This is a "on the trail" drink it there ever was one. I was informed of this drink while on a long trek through the Frank Church Wilderness. We stopped to pick some berries while hiking a high mountain trail looking for elk. Before I knew it my buddy had a plastic bottle of vodka in his hand and was begging me to take a plug off the top. Not being one to refuse booze, and my legs asking for it, I obliged. After about a quarter of the vodka was gone he started filling the bottle with huckleberries.

Yes, we quoted Val Kilmer as "Doc" Holliday, I think that you have to quote that movie when picking huckleberries. As you can see the recipe is simple – vodka, a trail and huckleberries.

Mulberry Infused Wine

Here we go round the mulberry bush,
The mulberry bush,
The mulberry bush.
Here we go round the mulberry bush
So early in the morning.

English Nursery Rhyme

Mulberries grow on trees, that much I know. This whole mulberry bush stuff is silly. What I also know is that they are delicious. I am always amazed to see purple-stained ground near a mulberry tree, often in the middle of major metropolitan areas. It's like no one knows that these berries are so tasty, or they just don't care.

Cobblers and crisps are often the end result of my mulberry picking. The trick with picking them is not to be gentle and grab one berry at a time. I like to spread a sheet, one you have no value in, on the ground below the tree. Then I shake the fruit-laden branches and watch as the fruit falls. Don't have on a white t-shirt while doing this, it will be purple when you are done. Trust me.

After I get the berries I want I will add them to cheap red wine at a party, kind of like sangria. I'll mash up some of the berries and then leave the rest whole in the bottom of a pitcher. On the top of the berries goes a sweet, cheap, red wine. You feel a little sophisticated but not that much. This is great for hot days and with an ice cube or two in the glass. Don't judge, it is delicious.

38

DESSERTS

Chocolate Shortbread

Shortbread is a weakness for me. I will eat every last crumb, and often end up with a stomach ache to prove it. This recipe is a prime example of why, chocolate and delicious I can't seem to keep it out of my mouth. Serve with some ice cream and a little elderberry bourbon and it is pure bliss.

Serves 5

8 oz. butter (2 sticks), room temperature
½ cup powdered sugar
2 cups all-purpose flour
½ teaspoon baking powder
2 oz. unsweetened chocolate, melted
½ teaspoon vanilla extract

Combine all ingredients, knead with hands to combine. Press into lightly buttered pans (or roll out to ½-inch thickness on a floured board and cut into shapes). Bake at 325°F for about 20 minutes. Cut into wedges while warm or break apart.

Tuscan Polenta Apricot Rum Cake

Classically-trained chefs are divided into two camps – hot food guys and bakers. Hot food chefs are the ones that get all the love. We are the ones you see, with the rare exception, on the Food Network making grilled dishes and doing sauté work. As a rule hot food guys are less technical than their baking brethren. Cooking is more about how things "feel" than how exact the measurement is.

Bakers do not function in the same way. Things are prescribed by a recipe. An exact amount of yeast is needed – too much and the bread will blow up, too little and it won't rise. That is why recipes from baker chefs are typically better than recipes from hot chefs.

My training is on the hot food side of the kitchen. I never enjoyed baking, not even a little. During interviews (chefs tend to change jobs a lot) I was often asked how I would handle the bakery aspect of the kitchen. My answer: "I will hire that talent."

Not being a baker but teaching a lot of cooking classes led me to this recipe. It lets me make a "cake" by feel.

Serves 6

3 cups milk
1 cup cream
½ cup (or more) medium or coarse-ground polenta
¼ cup bold flavored honey
2 teaspooons vanilla extract
½ cup dried apricots, chopped into slivers
¼ cup golden raisins, soaked for 20 minutes in ¼ cup light or dark rum

In a large, heavy saucepan bring milk and cream to a boil over medium heat. Whisk in polenta and continue whisking until it starts to thicken, 5-7 minutes. Add honey, lower heat and cook, stirring frequently, until thick, about 20 minutes. Remove from heat and stir in vanilla, apricots, raisins, and rum. Pour mixture into a 10-inch springform pan.
Tap against the counter to make the top level and smooth out the top using a spatula if necessary.

Cool to room temperature and serve.

The consistency of this cake is quite soft, not much like a "real" cake, but more like a pudding. It's good by itself, or you can serve it with an apricot puree.

Apricot and Cherry Cobbler

Nothing beats homemade cobbler. A time comes at the restaurant each year where I make a pie. That pie never really turns out the way I envisioned it and I end up with an inedible hunk of goop. Never one to admit defeat I change my mind and make a cobbler. Those, my friends, turn out wonderfully. Serve this one with ice cream.

Serves 6

2 cups fresh apricots, split and pits removed
2 cups fresh cherries, split and pits removed
½ cup sugar
1 cup plus pinch all-purpose flour
½ cup rolled oats
1 teaspoon salt
2 tablespoons baking powder
1 tablespoon lemon juice and zest
½ cup butter
¾ cup half and half

Preheat the oven to 375°F.

Combine apricots, sugar, and cherries in bowl. In another bowl mix the dry ingredients and the zest. Cut the butter into the dry ingredients and add the half and half to form a batter. Pour the fruit into a pie mold and top with batter.

Bake for 25-30 minutes. Serve warm.

ACKNOWLEDGMENTS

Hattie King, without you this book could never have happened. Based on the volume and variety of dead things that have been on our kitchen counter I cannot begin to express how grateful and blessed I am to be with such a tolerant and supportive wife. What we have created together is the highlight of my life. Each day I look to our three boys for inspiration —Noah, thank you for being so strong yet so kind. Cameron, you are made of pure-hearted gold and are the sweetest thing. Jordan, your four-year-old logic makes me examine my priorities; I strive to love things as passionately as you do.

Diane and Larry King are simply the best and most supportive parents ever. Mom, thank you for pheasant noodle soup and being demanding. Both of those things have had an outsized effect on my life. Dad, thank you for teaching me to hunt and to cook. This book is all your fault.

Ryan, thank you for teaching me how to be a line dog, how to think deep thoughts and for going on countless adventures with me. Mac you have always kept me in check and still offered unconditional friendship, I am eternally grateful. Jamie Allen, drop everything, I have an idea and it will be fun. I promise. Thank you Amy Atkins for refusing slop, asking for a better draft, and pushing me to be a better writer. Deanna Darr you have always been kind and supportive, even when I didn't deserve it. Andy Walgammot I can't believe you have been publishing these red-neck chef stories and recipes for the past four years. Hank Shaw thanks for being a mentor in this odd-ball hunting-fishing-cooking-writing career. You didn't have to open up to some fan-boy from Idaho, but you did and I am better for it.

Thank you Caxton Press and Scott Gipson for taking a chance on my idea.

A special thank you to Jocelyn Robertson for making *Chef in the Wild* more beautiful and clear than I could have ever hoped.

— Randy King
CHEF IN THE WILD

The following articles that have been previously published are as follows:

"One More Step Back," appeared in *Outdoor Life.*

"Eyes of a Hunter," appeared in *Edible Idaho.*

"Lessons from the Goose Blind," "Sage, Sage Grouse," "Eat the Carp," "Idaho Kitty Fish," "Eat the Invaders," "Snails," "Frogger" and "City Fishing" appeared in *Boise Weekly.*

"Turkey: Never as Planned," "Making Prairie Grizzlies Taste Good," and "Bring Home the Bacon" appeared in *Traditional Bowhunter Magazine.*

"Alaskan Dream" appeared in *Alaska Sporting Journal.*

"Game On," "The Someday Goose," "Armchair Quail Hunters," "Loathsome Dove," "Peaches and Cream Grouse," "The Lunch Break Chukar," "Seasoning After the Season," "The Between Season," "A Boy and His Bunny," "Rabbit Slam," "To My Shoulder in Elk," "Liver and Onions," "Anti-Loap," "Lessons on Whitetail Hunting from a Mule Deer Hunter," "Venison Meatloaf," "Best Backstrap Ever," "The Perfect Venison Backstrap," "City Folk Steelhead," "The $50 Crappie," "Half-Shell Bass," "Tuna," and "How Not to Catch Surfperch" appeared in *Northwest Sportsman Magazine.*

For a free catalog of Caxton titles write to:

Caxton Press
312 Main Street
Caldwell, ID 83605-3299

or

Visit our Internet website:

www.caxtonpress.com

Caxton Press is a division of The Caxton Printers, Ltd.